MAKE
YOUR
MONDAYS
MATTER

DISCOVER THE SECRETS TO PROPEL
YOUR BUSINESS TO THE NEXT LEVEL

JO JAMES

Published by Goldcrest Books International Ltd
www.goldcrestbooks.com
publish@goldcrestbooks.com

ISBN: 978-1-911505-47-1
eISBN: 978-1-911505-48-8

This book is for you.
To help you take those steps to bring your ideas to life. I'm cheering you on from here, propelling you to grow your business, one Monday at a time. You can do it!

To your success and happiness,

Jo James

"A great read for anyone who wants to banish those Monday morning blues and is looking for practical ideas to make every day, and every moment, really count. Written in a positive and conversational style, Jo shares her experience on how to create the right mindset to achieve your personal and business goals. There are lots of tools and tips that you can instantly try out for yourself and the book is structured so that it is really easy to dip in and out.

I love Jo's personable style and felt that she was right there with me, cheering me on as I read the book, speaking to me, encouraging me and supporting me to propel my business to the next level. She had me engaged right from the very start of the book that the tools and approach she has uncovered, can help me to increase sales for my businesses by a factor of 10!"

Maila Reeves, Entrepreneur, Angel Investor, Business Lecturer at Westminster Business School

"What better way to start your week? Monday morning blues is a thing of the past since 'Make Your Mondays Matter'! The author gives motivation and inspiration in plenty to lighten your load and lift your spirits. Her style of writing is personal, jovial and from the heart which we can all relate to.

... she will not only help you achieve incredible results but also methodically help to turn things around when they've gone pear-shaped.

Being a sole business owner can be lonely at times and we all need a boost of motivation, so that we never give up on the dream! 'Make Your Mondays Matter' certainly provides this and much more."

Cheryl Carter, Every Home Matters

"Woohoo... In the first 16 pages of 'Make Your Mondays Matter' by business coach and author, Jo James, you get a real sense of pace. This lady doesn't let the grass grow under her feet. If you're serious about being a creative entrepreneur, growing your business and making money then this is the book for you.

'Make Your Mondays Matter' is like having Jo as your coach but most importantly she's your business cheerleader! By encouraging you to keep going, take action and believe in yourself.

For me, this is a handbook I will refer to again and again. The questions and exercises are challenging enough to make a difference. Jo's guidance as a coach comes through. Most importantly it is the constant encouragement, the optimistic voice of someone who believes in my success that makes this book a winner.

Highly recommended if you're a creative entrepreneur ready to make a difference, grow your business and make some money."

Sharon Simpson, Dark Romantix

"Jo James gave me the motivation to make it happen and by following the easy to implement productivity tips and processes I immediately felt much more positive about my business and what I needed to do to make it really fly."

Wil Watts, Madam Geneva & Gent Gin Experiences

"Love your 'Make your Mondays Matter' book as there is always something I can take action on and it's all very doable too. I do what it suggests and it's become a lovely habit now and my business says thank you too"

Heather Waring, Women Walking Women Talking

"'Make Your Mondays Matter' is full of simple and illuminating tips to help you with starting a business, overcoming an obstacle or powering your business to the next level.

Reading the book has helped me in times of stagnation or when I feel overwhelmed. It also gives me the courage and the knowledge to continue my journey to expand my business to its full potential."

Emma Parker, Coutours

"Jo is a fantastic business coach and this book makes her accessible to more people. It is full of practical, no nonsense advice for growing your business, all done with a sense of humour. Jo (and this book) really help you to think about what you want to achieve in your business and gives you the tools to go about it, including everything from specific mindset and sales tips through to managing your time effectively.

Reading her book will definitely propel you into action to achieve what you want to."

Joanna Gaudoin, Inside Out Image

"Jo James is a wonderful declutterer of minds. She helps you make sense of it all with support, advice and guidance. Her clear structure and clear thinking will guide you on the route to achieve your success."

Andrew Rumbles, Prospera Wealth Management

"Secrets revealed here are essential to any successful business."

Luiz Peres, Elior Group General Manager.

CONTENTS

LET'S
GO

INTRODUCTION

Make Your Mondays Matter

Are you experiencing peaks and troughs in your income? Are you looking for proven systems and processes for business growth? If you're a Solopreneur or small business owner looking for proven ways to grow your existing business or make more money in your Start-up, then this book is for you.

This is a step-by-step 'how to' guide, propelling you to create a successful 6-figure business and beyond, and importantly to feel good along the way.

I believe in your potential, I believe you have great talents and skills and I'm here to help you take action and make some serious money! Sound good to you?

If you haven't got a business background, as many entrepreneurs haven't when they start out, then you're going to run into the age-old, typical problems of always trying to find clients, not knowing how to create a regular income, or worse, have a cash flow problem and not be able to trade any more. I don't want that to happen to you. I've got your back.

From turning around businesses to growing my own businesses over the last 25 years, I understand what it takes to start, develop and grow a successful business to multiple 6 and 7 figures. It's a rollercoaster of emotions, energy, successes and failures.

Business is certainly fun when it's all working out well with happy staff and customers, consistent incoming revenue, achieving and exceeding targets; it feels great. With the right systems and processes in place, it works.

Sometimes it can also feel quite lonely. Being the business owner, you have ALL the responsibility to make sure *everything* is done; your marketing, your business development, sales, networking, accounts *and* making sure you have happy customers and staff.

However, if you're always trying to work things out on your own, it can get overwhelming, tiring and deflating if you're not seeing enough results and revenue from your efforts.

That's why 10 years ago, I started and grew my second business, AmberLife VIP Business Coaching, to empower business owners just like you to get sales-savvy and implement proven systems to create their 6- (and 7-) figure business, and enjoy it!

When business networking I met so many people who were brilliant at what they do, but through no fault of their own as it wasn't needed in their creative roles, they did not have any sales training or a business background. Many people asked me for advice;

"How do you get your clients?"
"Where do you network?"

"What systems do you use?"
"How have you stayed in business for so long?"
"Can you help me please?"

The business owners I met were all brilliant at what they did. So passionate to start and grow their business, but I noticed there was one major element that they needed in their kit bag! Sales activity. So I organised, promoted and delivered a sales workshop to the business owners I had met networking and they loved it.

Seeing business owners have their 'Aha' moments around the table, I guided them to bust their beliefs around money and sales, and I gave them the exact strategy and systems and focused mindset I had used to build my businesses, which are the ones I'm giving you too.

Susan, the owner of a Virtual Assistant agency, attended my second Myth Busting Sales Boosting Workshop as she was experiencing peaks and troughs in her income and wasn't growing her business at the speed she wanted.

Another attendee described how I "make sales easy" by sharing *what* to do *when* and *how often*. After the workshop Susan felt so much more confident and implemented my sales strategy as soon as she got back to her office. Within 28 days she won 5 new clients totalling £11,000.

How much would that mean to you if you won 5 new clients in 28 days?

Susan has kept up the monthly momentum and using my Sales Strategy, she had doubled her business in revenue 12 months later *and* her team has grown to 10.

Inspired by so many of my private clients' successes, I want to share these strategies, techniques and proven client-winning ways so you too can thrive, not just survive. I want you to be wildly successful and live the life of your dreams.

I'll guide you every step of the way and encourage you to do just that!

I've taken what I know best from my 25 years of being in business and honed these techniques to deliver them with crystal clear clarity so you can take action and realise *your* dreams. Delivered here for you in manageable chunks.

Running a successful business takes dedication and commitment and a good dose of self-belief and confidence. But most of all it takes action.

When you take regular action you will learn valuable lessons and get valuable feedback. You will find clients, supporters, raving fans and ambassadors for your business who will help you sell your services too.

This book has been written and designed as a business planner on steroids. Within these pages are my secrets of success, top time-management tips and winning sales techniques to help you create *your* 6-figure business, and importantly with a mindset boost too, you will feel good along the way.

I have given you space to keep your notes and ideas in one place.

I'll give you clear action steps every single Monday.

Take action on a Monday and you'll get more results by Friday. Taking *consistent* action is what's needed for success. Throughout the year, you will gain traction on your dreams, implement proven systems and processes to make more sales and feel confident to win more business.

Why Make Your Mondays Matter?

Monday is usually the day of the week when you may feel like you're starting over again, saying to yourself, 'oh no it's Monday, what am I going to do this week? Where am I going to get more business from? More clients? What shall I do to boost my revenue?'

So instead of asking those questions each week, you will have answers as you read this book. You'll have time each Monday to work *on your* business and enjoy the feeling of making headway on your goals. My clients love this! By setting themselves up well on a Monday, getting sales activity started, social media and networking planned, they feel more productive and in control. They've worked *on* their business, not just *in* it.

You will then have the rest of the week to make progress on your goals and work with your clients knowing you have done something constructive to grow your business every week.

This book will guide you, inspire you and give you clear Action Points so that you 'make it happen' and get more results every Friday. Imagine how good that will feel. You'll always have something to celebrate every Friday. Just in case you needed an excuse, ha ha!

You will have me coaching and supporting you every Monday to develop your business. You will become more confident, make more money and achieve the goals that are important to you. We will take small steps every week and keep building on your skills and experience to create your thriving business.

Whether you feel ready or not, get ready for the ride of your life. And I'll be right by your side.

I promise that I'm going to make this as easy as I can for you. You'll be amazed at how fast you can get results, once you're focused and consistently taking action.

I predict that within 3 months you'll have made more money than before and probably doubled or even tripled your income within 12 months.

And by following these steps and taking action you will have opened many more doors, met many more people and created many more opportunities for future growth.

You will have clarity, feel confident and gain more clients.

MD Angela, who owns a water purifying business came to my Sales Workshop as she wanted to refresh her sales skills and learn how to take her business to the next level. By using the #1 method I will share with you, Angela earned an EXTRA £130,000 in 10 months, and a year later had built a thriving 7-figure business. All by consistently implementing my sales strategies and techniques to win new business and gain *repeat* business.

And I'm going to share it all with YOU.

I've written some of this book from my villa in the Algarve in Portugal where I work with clients online from my office overlooking the pool. I commute each month between Portugal and London to work face to face with my clients and facilitate my networking events. Working and living in two countries has always been my dream. Well, mine and my husband's! I haven't told you that to impress you, but to inspire you that it *is all* possible.

I don't have a university degree. I left school at 16 after my career counsellor introduced me to my then dream job, working in a laboratory. After being successful on interview I left my A-levels after one term. I wanted to progress in the company and become a developer of new products, so I went on to study analytical chemistry for 1 year, which I so wish I could remember now!

After happily being there for nearly 4 years, I heard rumours the company was closing down, so it was time to move, and there it was, an advert in the local newspaper asking me if I'd like to run a pub. Well it wasn't written to me personally, but would I like to run a pub? Hell yeah! I went from Bristol to London and was successful in securing the trainee managerial position and worked in a huge pub called The Chandos with my bedroom overlooking Trafalgar Square. I fell in love with London immediately.

After getting through the training, at 23, I started in my first pub, The Canonbury Tavern in Islington, London, with my first husband. We took it from £1500 a week to £15,000 a week in 9 months. Yes you read right, from £1500 to £15,000 – that's 10 times more in sales every week! Would you like to do that too? We built a great team behind the bar to deliver excellent customer service to ensure we had repeat business.

From growing the business to £750,000 in one year, I was hooked on growing businesses and turning them around to make a good profit.

As part of making the business successful, I updated the restaurant area and in time, cooked for 50 people every day. It was great fun. After smashing through our sales targets and achieving £¾ million in turnover each year we received a huge bonus of £40,000. Being 25, that was a LOT of money to me.

With this bonus in hand, we decided to go travelling and visit America, Australia and Asia. We planned a fantastic round the world trip for 12 months. I love meeting new people and immersing myself into new cultures, eating new foods and exploring our beautiful world. It was an amazing experience I will never forget and I learned so much along the way. We travelled around America, Fiji, Australia for 9 months and eventually arrived in Hong Kong and while there, applied for a visa to cross the border into China.

Seeing China before her transformation was incredible. When I was in Shanghai in 1990, there was just one KFC, the only Western shop in the whole of China. The street lights went out at 7pm and we were encouraged to only eat in our hotel in the evenings. Times have changed since then.

We returned to England slightly ahead of schedule as war had broken out in the Middle East. There always seems to be a war somewhere, sadly. When we heard the news, we were staying on the gorgeous Phi Phi Island in Thailand but were advised to leave quickly to catch a plane, to guarantee we'd get home.

Once back in Britain, I picked up the phone to our previous area manager who was thrilled to hear from me and invited us to view a pub in Barnstaple, Devon, South England. It had a 50-seater restaurant upstairs which my area manager knew would entice me, and a skittle alley that I turned into a live music venue. We also had 7 letting rooms, and I know from managing them, I never want to run a hotel!

We had that pub for nearly 3 years doubling the turnover from £600,000 to £1.2 million in our first year of being there. Business was great.

But then, as often happens, at 28 I wanted to change my life. I felt unfulfilled in my personal relationship and decided I wanted to go back to London to pursue more dreams by myself. It was a hard time and I felt under pressure to do what conventionally I *should* do, stay. Not what I *wanted* to do, which was to leave. So after a good six months of upset and constantly questioning myself, I knew I had to be brave and leave my first husband.

Amazingly only 6 weeks later I met the man who was to become my second husband, Mark James. We were friends for 2 years before getting together as I needed some space and time to work in London and see where my plans took me. But you can't fight love. I'd found my soulmate, he's my best friend and we're still happily together 22 years on. Plus, I have 3 wonderful, clever, inspiring stepdaughters. And a few cats! It's been an amazing experience and I feel very grateful being able to see my stepdaughters grow up and be part of their lives and family.

In 1994 I worked as a retail manager for a leading health food brand, and then a sales manager at a leading frozen food company where I created a new revenue stream from scratch, totalling over £1 million in just a year.

But I wanted more of a challenge, more money, and a new career, so I joined the world of recruitment at 30 years old, working for Adecco, and absolutely thrived. My clients loved the fact that I had built my own teams before in my career so could relate to how important it is to get the right team.

A company is only truly as successful as the people in it. I learned brilliant interview techniques which helped me to discover *above* average performers, as opposed to average or below average, plus with my ability to spot potential in people, and knowing our clients inside and out, I was very good at finding the perfect match. For both my clients and my candidates.

There are so many coincidences in this world and you never know when you're going to bump into people again. I remember going for my second job interview in recruitment and during the interview she said, 'oh my, you worked in Barnstaple in Devon? You must have met my husband! He used to come in the pub nearly every day.' He was one of our best regulars. What a coincidence!

I love it when that happens and believe that we are connected in ways that scientists just can't prove yet as they haven't got the instruments to measure the connection. How do we know to say who's calling us on the phone sometimes, when we say, "I bet that's Andy on the phone," or your friend's name of course! How often do you say that? Is it coincidence? Energy? Or is it 'The Force'?

Do you find coincidences like that happen often? People come and go, but hopefully many like-minded people stay longer, and you'll develop great relationships during your lifetime.

I have learned that developing good solid relationships is paramount to success. And the good news is, sales is all about relationships.

At 35 I left the corporate world to start my own recruitment agency called Amber Associates. My first baby! My very own business. I'd made millions for other companies so I was confident I could make money for myself and my family now.

My entrepreneurial journey began and what a ride! Laughter and some tears, but mostly happy times.

I remember the first day very vividly. I'd quit my job and it was the Tuesday after the bank holiday, May 29th 2001. I was sitting at our dining room table with my shiny new PC, notebook and a phone.

I knew I had to start building new relationships with my ideal target market and meet new business owners. I was so excited!

With a vision, a plan of action, my target market and niche set, my recruiting skills learned from 5 years of working in the West End, City of London and the Docklands, I was ready to have my own business. I wanted to do it better, to give a better service, to have a better way of life. As I can imagine, you do too.

I was a start-up. Proud of joining the hundreds of thousands of other start-ups that year. I picked up the phone and started to call directors and human resource managers to see if they would like a new recruitment service, with a difference.

You've got to stand out from the crowd and deliver excellence. I'd had 5 years' recruitment experience coupled with 10 years management experience in hospitality and retail, so knew what it took to build a team and businesses to 6 and 7 figures, I understood my clients' situation and how important it is to take on the right staff.

I was successful in quickly finding 2 clients to work with and placed exceptional candidates in the roles so I was able to process invoices in my first few months. Things were going according to plan. But then in my fourth month, September 11th happened. The world was in shock. The City was like a ghost town, it was so very eerie, no one was around and some of my friends had lost their colleagues in New York. I remember talking to a director who was going to pack up and move back to the north of England, where he thought it would be safer. Fear was everywhere. No one was recruiting, so after a few weeks, I spent the time putting together some marketing material and created my first website.

We've got to keep going

September 11th was one of many challenging times and recessions I had to learn how to get through.

I was one recruiter amongst the 1200 recruitment consultants in a square mile in the City of London, I was told one day. So I was soon back at my desk, picking up the phone, reminding my clients "I am here, ready to help recruit for you". With a passion, hard work and the sheer determination that I was going to succeed in London, I picked up the phone time and time again. It worked.

Nine months in and I was able to rent my first office in Artillery Lane in the City of London near Spitalfields Market and employed a consultant. Brilliant, I had staff now. By the end of year 3, we moved again, into Devonshire Row, opposite Liverpool Street Station and employed an office manager, Jennifer, to join us. I loved that office. I loved my team. I loved my clients. I loved my Amber Temps. We got on famously and I'm still in touch with some of them today. Jennifer now has her own business in London, called Debutots.

We specialised in recruiting for Media companies, Finance and Medical Health. Focusing on providing great candidate care we quickly gained a reputation for looking after our candidates, spotting career opportunities for them, not just filling a job, and my business grew well. Candidates told their friends about us. Our clients gave us sole supply agreements as we saved them recruitment fees because we kept getting it right. The candidates we placed were promoted and they built their teams, and of course, called us first when looking to hire.

We still had competition, there is always competition. So you have to be proactive, solve problems, spot opportunities when they arise and act on them immediately, all while delivering excellent customer service and solutions to stand out from the crowd.

We were a good team and grew the business year on year by implementing my sales strategy and beating targets to multiple 6-figures. We were doing well and getting a great reputation for getting it right for our clients and our candidates. #Result

We worked so well together and helped hundreds of people with their next career move and helped build teams and businesses. The future was bright, Amber bright.

Then, I nearly lost everything

Just as I was about to invest in a 3-storey building a few doors away from our office in Devonshire Row, the financial crash came and I lost 75% of my business in about 3 weeks. Companies had a recruitment freeze on. Most of my temps' assignments ended quickly. It was horrible. No one knew what was going to happen. To make things even worse, thanks to my landlord, we had another horrible surprise, so I decided I was moving out and moving on. Why my landlord? From nowhere, with no warning, we were being threatened with having the electricity in the office cut off. Court letters arrived. Talks with lawyers started. Our landlord hadn't paid the electricity bill for 13 years. So with all things considered, I decided to move out and build my Amber empire, again. Well, after a 'Jo James is leaving the City' party!

AmberLife was born

At home, I turned our spare room into an office and continued to service my media clients who were based in the West End while I pursued my next career and passion, personal development. In November 2008 I passed my Master Practitioner NLP course with NLP Life Training and in January 2009 combined my new NLP skills with my recruitment and business skills and set up AmberLife to help business owners grow their business, launching on April 1st. Well you've got to keep your sense of humour, eh!

The networking scene had changed and due to the financial crisis, I kept meeting people who had been made redundant, or were overworked and were fed up with doing about 5 people's jobs so were setting up by themselves.

They were often taking me for coffee to 'pick my brains' and ask me, "where do you get your clients? When do I register for VAT? How did you do it?" etc.

They were great at what they did, were talented executives, web designers, photographers, trainers, consultants who weren't sure what to do next after being made redundant and PAs who wanted to become VAs. Through no fault of their own as it wasn't needed in their jobs and they hadn't run a business before, they didn't have any sales or marketing experience.

I knew I had to help them thrive in business. That was my driver, my purpose, which it still is to this day, to share all I know to help you grow your business, to stay in business and create a thriving business and be free to do what you want to do in life.

If I can do it, so can you!

Keep your vision in mind, keep taking action and you can bring your dreams to life.

Everyone's journey is different. From my 25 years of being highly successful in client facing and sales management roles and having grown 7 successful businesses, I want to share my secrets of success with you. Plus, due greatly to my hard work and commitment, I have helped hundreds of business owners to feel more confident, become sales savvy and work with more clients to create *their* profitable, successful businesses. Often doubling and trebling their business revenue each year we work together in my sales training workshops and coaching programs.

Would you like to double your revenue?

First, you need to put practical business systems into place and learn proven techniques to win new clients, get repeat business and *grow* your business.

You need to have a structure, a business development strategy *and* a business mindset or you're going to feel overwhelmed, and worn out.

If you're not making sales and don't have a steady income, you'll run out of money and you'll have to find another job. And you don't want that, do you? No, I thought not!

Building a business is much like building a house; you need to visualise the house of your dreams, get the foundations right and then you can build up and extend when you want to as your family grows.

Then the next step will be to turn your house into a home; implement a sales strategy to develop your sales cycle which will give you *recurring* revenue, *repeat* business and maximise new business opportunities when you see them. Yes, as you work through this book, you will be able to spot an opportunity easier too.

I remember one of my Mastermind Group clients, Nicola, a creative director, suddenly being aware of this opportunity-spotting skill. She was in a meeting with one of her suppliers who had popped into her office. He showed her some new materials she was interested in and then mentioned one of his other clients who was on her Top 10 of businesses she'd like to work with. Nicola was super interested then! After saying she would love to work with them too and before he left, he kindly made an introduction via LinkedIn for her. After meeting them, she had the opportunity to pitch for a £1 million project. My clients do love their Top 10, as I'm sure you will too!

Like a house with a beautifully designed interior, your business will look great and be a comfortable space for you to be in.

Well I say comfortable, being realistic, you'll need to do things that at first are *un*comfortable. Like anything new, as you are doing things for the first time, you need to step outside your comfort zone so often when you're running your own business. In fact it happens so many times a week, if not daily, I encourage you to become comfortable: being uncomfortable. I've found it's easier that way.

To propel your success I believe that you need to take consistent action and developing a focused business mindset will help you progress quicker and with more ease. You'll build resilience so that you are able to keep going, even when it's tough. Because in reality, there will be some tough times, tough days and some tough weekends! There may be times when your friends and family will be missing you. And you'll miss them.

You'll have some fears to conquer. There may well be tears. You'll have some limiting beliefs that are holding you back, which you'll find out as you go along, but the good news is we'll change those together for more powerful, *useful* beliefs. I bet your limiting beliefs are so last decade!

Sometimes you'll wonder why you ever started a business in the first place. We all do! It's totally normal and as entrepreneurs we experience so many ups and downs we must be mad to start in the first place. But we love it! And I'm sure you will too.

Because of course, there will be so many good times they will totally outweigh the tricky times and you'll work with great clients and I predict you'll have many celebrations.

You have your dreams and reasons why you want to have your own business. Both personally and professionally, you know what you want to achieve by growing your business? Maybe you want to own your first property, start a family, build a dream kitchen, go on holiday, live in two places, be number 1 in your sector, be the 'go-to' expert in your field?

In this book, I have created space for you to personally and professionally develop your business skills. It will be like walking into my AmberLife Mind Spa. A space created especially for you. A space where we'll meet and we'll talk about your business and I'll set you challenges with clear Action Points to help you take the next step. And the next. You'll learn to prioritise your time differently using my super-effective Time Management plan called The Power of 7.

I will be there helping you, encouraging you and will give you some amazing proven tools and techniques to help you through tricky times and on to good times. Anything can be done if you put your mind to it. We're all living proof of that, aren't we? I'm sure you've had challenges in the past, and have asked for advice, so I'm pleased to meet you and love that you have taken the time to buy this book and grow your business. Thank you. I look forward to working with you via these pages.

How to use this book

The book is divided into four sections which represent the four quarters of the financial year. Each section has a main theme and you can jump into any section that you want to focus on. The four sections are:

Make Your Sales Matter
Make Your Networking Matter
Make Your Mindset Matter
Make Your Year Matter

Each section is divided into weeks and every Monday you can open this book to find goal setting exercises and clear Action Points to keep you on track to building and growing your business. You can review your progress as you make notes within this book, record your achievements and see how far you've come.

Your first session will look at your vision for your business and please, make sure it's big! You'll be amazed at what you can achieve. I'm then going to share some tools with you to help you get more organised. Then I will give you Action Points to build your momentum and business, one Monday at a time.

You can start at the beginning of the book and read through to the end or you can read one section and then implement the Action Points I've outlined for you that day which are proven to help you win more clients. Or you can dip in and out of the book as you choose. It's up to you but please do read this book, make notes in it, maybe even put it in your bag and take it with you on your commute. It's yours and it's all written to help you grow your business and enjoy doing it!

Remember, come back to this book every Monday and there will be a Business Growth exercise with clear Action Points, propelling you to take action.

You can revisit and review as much as you like and turn this book into your own business growth planner.

Yes you're going to take risks, yes you're going to do things you thought were impossible, but in hindsight, you'll probably think that they were actually the most exciting times. Tell other people. Your stories and experience will inspire other business owners who were once in your position, to do the same.

To take that step and go for it, be in charge of your own destiny is actually quite exhilarating and freeing. Making your own decisions that will shape your future and your life is empowering.

Do it.

After all, we only live once, this isn't a dress rehearsal!

What do you want to achieve?

With your new ideas to develop your business, I can feel your excitement and maybe a little apprehension or nervousness too? I'd love to now give you the belief that it's all going to work out well.

Because you may as well think it *will* work out well. Developing a positive business mindset will also be key to your success. Being more in control of your own mind, rather than it controlling you, will make a difference to how much you enjoy your journey to success, and it's healthier too!

You have the choice as to what you think about, which has a direct effect on how you feel. Think about that for a minute. Read it again.

Those thoughts in turn will affect the quality of the actions that you then take, which will determine your results.

Imagine it all working out well.

This will put you in a more energising, determined, focused and happier mindset which will help you achieve your goals with more ease.

So many business owners I know have successfully built their business to 6-figures and beyond and are happier along the way. You'll learn to eat your carrots! I'll explain more about that later.

It does take your commitment and drive to realise your dreams and the most important things it takes to become a reality are your determination, commitment and consistent action.

Now with the best will in the world, without talking to people, be it online or offline, without telling people you exist and without sales activities, sales being THE most vital skill you need, you won't have a business in years to come. You'll have a very expensive hobby.

Stay with me, remember the good news. Sales is all about relationships, so no need to shy away.

Sales activity is THE most important element to put into the mix. Sales activity will make your networking work smarter for you. Sales activity will give you a bigger return on your marketing as you'll be able to close (we talk about how to do this later) for the business after you've received enquiries and leads from your marketing efforts, time and spend.

In this book are THE SECRETS on how to sell, **the *anti-selling way.***

Without action though, nothing will be achieved. Your ideas will stay as just thoughts, and we'll all miss out on your brilliance and expertise and what you have to offer to improve our lives. And you don't want that, do you?

I'll be here with you every step of the way. You have me on your side. Encouraging you. Guiding you. Cheering you on from here.

Helping you to regularly get out of your own way so you take action, I'll keep you on track with targets that you'll grow to love as you see your results soar.

So, settle in, grab a cuppa and let's get started.

It's you and me now, all the way.

Let's go!

GET STARTED AND GET ORGANISED

What ideas do you have bubbling away to grow your business?

Is there a product or service that's still an idea that you have been toying with but not yet started due to one reason or another?

What challenge or new project would you like to start now?

➠ Never underestimate the talents that you have. I bet you do though. Stop it!

➠ Never underestimate the potential that you can offer others. I bet you do though. Stop it!

➠ Never underestimate what you can do if you put your mind to it. I bet you do though. Stop it!

Just imagine now that you have started your project and have a good revenue-generating client from it, how would that make you feel?

Excited? Proud? Pleased with yourself? How will you feel? Write it down in the space on the next page.

How do I feel?

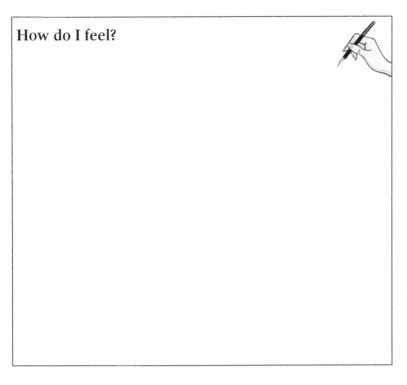

I predict you will love the challenges, the energising pressure of your new commitments, the secret delights of those stressful moments, all those quirky creative kinks we share!

First, let's create a clear vision for your business.

Make a note of where you are now. What revenue have you generated so far this year? Write it down here.

Revenue so far this year...

Now, fast forward to 12 months' time. What revenue do you want to have achieved by this time next year? Write it down here.

Revenue by this time next year...

It will be great to be able to look back to today and see where you were when you started and see how much revenue you have created by the end of the year.

If you're stuck for revenue generating ideas or want to try something new to help you to create a brighter future, here's my favourite visualisation technique to help you think big.

Come on a helicopter ride with me!

This is one of THE most powerful 5 step visualisation exercises to get your creative juices flowing. See what you discover.

Ready?

Good.

Now, enjoy the ride!

1. Write down your financial target for the next 3 months...

> **My financial target for the next 3 months is...**
>
>

Maybe you've written a target of £5,000 or £20,000, whatever works for you. Remember to multiply by 4 to get your annual revenue.

2. Now, add a zero to the quarterly target, so as in this example, it will now be £50,000 or £200,000. Hmm, I bet that feels more exhilarating, doesn't it? You might well be thinking, what do you need to do *differently* to achieve your new boosted goal? So now imagine...

3. Stepping inside your virtual helicopter, fasten your seat belt and let's go for a ride and think big to get ideas on how you can *achieve* your new boosted goal. You may want to read through this exercise first, then come back to this point, close your eyes and let your imagination do the work for you.

4. Imagine flying high above your desk and as you ascend higher, past the roof of your house, higher so you can see an area much wider below you. Rise again and see the land, your country, and more, as a bird sees it. Fly higher so you get that aerial view.

5. Let the power of your imagination help you to see where it's taking you. With your new financial target in mind, get creative on how you're going to achieve that.

6. Looking out of the helicopter window, what can you see yourself doing? Are you online talking to camera to your desired audience across the globe? Are you speaking on stage to hundreds of people? Are you hosting a local radio station?

    Who are you talking to? Where are you networking to meet more people?

    What have you just thought of that might sound like a crazy idea at first, but is probably the thing that will get you there?

    Where are you going? Are you collaborating, joining forces with someone?

    Meeting up? Getting on stage? Writing a book?

    What are you doing differently?

    Write down your ideas as they appear to you. You can use the space over the page if you wish.

    You might have just seen a brilliant idea before your very eyes as to ways and new avenues that you can take.

    When you are ready, come down to earth gently and sit back into your seat in your office or wherever you started from feeling refreshed, revitalised and raring to go!

My helicopter ride...

Excellent. From completing the Helicopter Ride exercise you now have new ideas on how to generate more revenue.

Set your internal Sat Nav.

This will help take the ideas you had on your helicopter journey and set your direction.

Let's get specific on one goal at a time.

Choose one of those big goals you just discovered on your helicopter ride.

Imagine that you have already achieved your goal. Yes, that's right, fast forward in your mind to the time when you have completed your goal.

Imagine what that will be like. How do you feel?

What new things do you see?

What do you hear around you?

Notice what you notice – write your thoughts on page 42.

There may be some hidden insights that appear as you are now in the future, in that wonderful place of hindsight. How many times have you heard people say, I wish I had known that when I started?

Now you can answer your own question, and, if you were asking, yes you can travel in time!

As you imagine yourself in the future, what do you want to tell yourself in the present?

When I do this exercise with my clients, their future selves often say to their present selves...

"You can do it. Believe in yourself.
Keep taking action and you'll do it!"

My internal Sat Nav...

Then when you are ready, in your mind's eye, turn and look back to where you started and see what events took place for you to get where you are now.

Notice what you notice.

What important events do you see happening?

Who is around you?

What do you need to do first?

Have you just reprioritised some tasks to do in different months from what you first thought? What do you need to do next?

Now, come back to the present moment again, with all that additional knowledge of the future.

Remember to write down any new information that you have discovered. There is space opposite for that.

Take a deep breath and allow your learnings to integrate into you, whatever that means to you.

And take another deep breath. In. And out. And again. In. And out. Good.

Well done! You have just set your own internal Sat Nav. and created new neural pathways.

Now you have travelled there once, to where you will be when you have achieved your goals, it will be easier for your brain to help you get there again.

As with a Sat Nav in a car, you have set yourself a new direction to help you on your journey of success.

Smile – to let your brain know this is good for you!

Each time you smile you release good chemicals; serotonin, dopamine, endorphins.

These help to counteract the toxic chemicals like cortisol, which we naturally produce when we are stressed.

No wonder smiling is good for you! Even if you force a smile, or if you remember a time when you were with your friends and had a good belly laugh, as you giggle again, and smile, your body will thank you.

I recommend you have a big glass of water now. You've done so well and if we were together in the same room, like my clients, I'd give you a high five, and probably a hug!

Well done from me. You rock!

Talking of creating neural pathways...

New neural pathways are created when you learn. By repeating the same action, it's like the neural pathway creates a groove in your brain, which by repetition gets stronger and deeper.

By *repeating* things in life, our neural pathways help us to form habits, be they helpful, or not. Remember when you first tried to ride a bike or drive a car? How you had to think about every move, every gear change, and probably made mistakes. This is called 'conscious incompetence'.

Then, after a period of time, you practised and repeated the learning to ride over and over again until you could cycle without falling or found that driving was more natural. You didn't have to keep thinking about pressing down the clutch pedal before you changed gear. You just did it! And you got to where you wanted to.

It felt more natural to you. This is called 'unconscious competence'. And is where you had strengthened the neural pathways.

To get to 'unconscious competence' quicker, visualise yourself doing what you want to achieve more often.

This is why visualisation techniques work so well to help you prepare for what you are about to do. We know athletes visualise running the marathon. During their training regime they also take time to imagine themselves running round the route. Pacing themselves, they can see themselves breathing, they breathe along with the visualisation, they imagine themselves running through that 'wall', successfully, seeing how they got through that challenge and kept going, breathing well again, running strong to the end of the race, so that when the day comes, the brain has already been trained to focus on what you want to achieve.

When you start your day, imagine it all working out well and specifically note what you want to achieve by the *end* of the day.

➠ What will you see?
➠ What will you hear?
➠ How will you feel?

By activating your sensory connections and visualising what you want to achieve, your brain will know where you want it to go, and it will get there easier for you, and help you on your way. Isn't that clever!

Often when I meet clients during the first session, after we've done the Helicopter Ride exercise to help them think big and set their internal Sat Nav, we then look at how they are organising their day and week.

So, now let's create new effective time management habits for you to work with, to create results, with more ease, and more time.

It's time to chunk down your goals and make your schedule work for you.

Let me show you these 3 brilliant ways of organising your day. You'll love them!

1. The Power of 7

To help you turn your big goals into tasks you can do, let's now look at this powerful way to help you break down your day into manageable chunks of time and prioritise how you are organising your day.

My clients love this method. It helps you turn your big ideas into actions. Entrepreneurs are usually never short of ideas! That's what makes it fun and makes us who we are, but it's by taking consistent action on our goals that we create a sustainable and profitable business. And that's what you want too, isn't it?

The Power of 7 is the name one of my clients, Linda, a Senior Financial Advisor gave it, and she was so spot-on with the name! Why? Because your brain is able to comfortably remember 7 things, plus or minus 2. You might have heard of this before.

You are also in different energy zones during the day as you complete different tasks as you need different powers of concentration or creativity to focus and complete things.

The Power of 7 will help you to be more productive and have some energy left at the end of the day to go out with your friends or partner for the evening or enjoy some quality family time. Go to the gym, eat out, or do whatever you want to. Sound good to you?

Often, when clients first start working with me, they feel like they're running around but not finishing things they want to and getting overwhelmed thinking about taking even more work on.

They're busy answering emails, going from one thing to another, phoning people, then emailing them, then getting caught up in their inbox and then it's lunchtime and they still haven't completed what they set out to do.

I liken this to circular cleaning. If you ran from room to room, starting off in your bedroom, making the bed but then found a couple of cups, running down the stairs to the kitchen, then you washed up, then found some receipts that should be in your home office, or desk area, so you go to that room, then you see your jumper, so you run to your bedroom again. And so on. Running from room to room but not finishing tidying any of the rooms and you're a hot sticky mess after a couple of hours. Not surprising! That's exactly how I used to clean my house. Not anymore!

Running from room to room is like going from emails to phone call, back to emails, going online to do research for a client, back to your emails, and so on. Whoa, are you feeling worn out or fed up just reading that? I'm not surprised!

You would be more effective cleaning and tidying one room at a time. As in your workload, you will be able to complete more work by focusing on one activity at a time.

By focusing on ONE activity at a time: for example, phoning everyone you need to, BEFORE you open your inbox to send them what you promised, you will get through your phone calls quicker. You will remain 'in the zone' and have better conversations. And you won't get distracted by all the other emails that you've seen!

So, do all your emails in one go, after your phone calls.

Then do the next chunk of activity. Maybe it's research, or working on a design or doing your accounts. Each takes different powers of concentration. Which is why it is more favourable to focus on ONE activity at a time for a longer period of time, helping you stay focused.

So, rather than having a long to-do list, separate the list into different types of activities.

I have included the Power of 7 template on page 50 for you to use in planning out your day. Instead of using a to-do list transfer your list into boxes of specific activity. Specific, focused brain power.

As you can see there are eight boxes. Each box will have one chunk of activity. For example, I usually use these 8 chunks:

1. phone calls

2. emails

3. research online for example, looking at client websites from enquiries

4. writing – includes blogs, feature articles and my newsletter I write for my community of brilliant business owners.

Then the next 4 boxes are:

5. images – choosing pictures for social media and blogs

6. accounts admin

7. what do I need to prepare for client meetings?

8. I leave this box free or sometimes put a smiley face! So at all times during the day I can see white space, giving me time to breathe and relax. Plus, if I get an unexpected call that needs my attention by the end of business that day, I write it in box 8, so I can easily see and prioritise it.

What chunks of time are important for you to include?

Yes, you can change them daily, weekly, depending on what projects and client work you need to complete.

I usually keep 6 boxes the same but change 2 when I need to.

Your Action Point today is to write out your Power of 7 and at first take one hour for each chunk and see how you feel after your *focused* activity, instead of running round the house going from room to room, getting worn out quickly!

Schedule the rest of the chunks into your online calendar. I schedule everything in my calendar. If it's scheduled, it gets done.

So, use the Power of 7 today, turn off all distractions and notice how you feel at the end of the day and how much more you've achieved.

To make your Mondays matter, get rid of that to-do list.

The Power of 7

2. Colour Code Your Day

I remember working with one of my Mastermind Group clients, Cheryl, a web designer, who dug her heels in for months before she implemented this method of organising her day. "Please implement it for four weeks," I asked her, "it truly works."

Before she started colour coding her day Cheryl felt overwhelmed with so much to do and was shying away from following up on leads because if she was successful at winning the business, she didn't know how she could design everyone's website at the same time.

By implementing the system to Colour Code her day, Cheryl can see when she can start work with new clients, and confidently give them their start date. She can see at a glance when she's out of the office at networking events or having meetings.

After sticking with this, Cheryl grew in confidence and by following the Top 10 too she has *trebled* her business revenue. That's a great #result!

Your Action Point today is to Colour Code Your Day.

Are you easily able to find the time to take on new client projects? Or like Cheryl used to be, are you already staying up 'til all hours and getting stressed out trying to finish it all?

Her desired outcome was to feel more in control, more relaxed and importantly, have the ability to take on more work, with ease.

So first, we looked at all the different chunks of time she needed using the Power of 7.

MAKE YOUR MONDAYS MATTER

For example do you need to have research time in your day? Do you need designing time? Writing proposal time? Client feedback time? Training time?

And then there's Networking time. Client meeting time. Sales Focused Time. Client Question time.

All these chunks of tasks and pockets of time to fit into your day.

No wonder it's easy to get overwhelmed with so much to do. Especially if you're looking at lists all day, and have lists of lists. Do you?

"Get rid of that to-do list" I said.

"Use your online calendar to schedule your workload instead."

How?

1. Chunk all the tasks you do to complete projects and client work
2. Colour Code your tasks (and stick to them long term)
3. Then schedule the individual chunks into your online calendar. One that syncs with your phone and laptop.
4. Remember to put in your sales activity time and admin time in different colours.

What chunks of time do you need in your day? Write them down in the space opposite.

What colour would you like to give each chunk?

For example, I have purple for client session time, yellow for meetings, networking and events so I can quickly see when I'm out of the office, orange for writing time, blogging, writing my newsletter and working on my business and blue is for business development and client calls.

At a glance I can see what my day, week or month's activities are.

So, if you feel like you're running out of time too often, use the Power of 7 to chunk down your big goals into manageable chunks of activity and Colour Code your diary.

Chunks of time I need each day...

3. What's your Most Important Thing?

If you're looking at your chunks of time, and are stuck with what to do first, ask yourself:

"What's the #1 Most Important Thing I need to do right now, to help me move towards my goal?"

I used to have this printed out and stuck to my wall!

If you are ever stuck during the day, overwhelmed or procrastinating, this is one of THE most powerful coaching questions to help you move towards your goals.

From now on, in this book, I will refer to this as your MIT. Your Most Important Thing. Your MIT. There is space in this book each week for you to write down your MIT.

Your Action Point today is to identify "What's THE #1 MIT you want to achieve this week?" Write it in the space opposite.

When you want to get something done, I recommend turning off all distractions.

Turn off your emails, turn your phone over so you can't see notifications and close all other tabs on your laptop.

➤ Focus ◄

➤ Do one thing at a time ◄

➤ Take one step at a time ◄

You'll feel great because you will have completed things by lunchtime and the end of the day, not just started 5 things and nothing's finished!

Being task focused one by one is the proven way forward to getting results.

Multi-tasking is so last decade! Focusing on ONE thing is a hot topic in business training right now. As I like to say...

MIT

What's the #1 Most Important Thing I need to do right now, to help me move towards my goal?

Focus is the new F-Word

We're now going to focus on one specific area of business for each quarter and I'm going to coach you on, yes, you've guessed it, every Monday, so you can work on your business every week. You'll feel great as you take action and make headway on *your* business growth and see more results.

QUARTER 1

MAKE YOUR SALES MATTER
AND Q1 GOALS

Get clarity and discover your sales superpowers.

MYMM 1.

SETTING GOALS FOR SUCCESS IN Q1

Your Action Point for today is to Set Your Goals for Quarter 1.

Why do I recommend working in Quarters?

All the companies I have ever worked with talk and refer to their business in Quarters. So I want to pass this on to you, so you get into the habit of using Quarters in your business too.

Business budgets and targets are usually spoken in Quarters. You may have heard others use 90 day plans, which similar in terms of time, but most companies and organisations use the term 'Quarters'.

In one year, there are 4 Quarters of 3 months or 13 weeks.

Q1 is January to March

Q2 is April to June

Q3 is July to September

Q4 is October to December

Many companies start Q1 in January while some companies have their first Quarter in April when their new budgets come out.

This book is written as if Q1 begins in January, but you can choose different Quarters to focus on one area of your business or pick a Monday that interests you and start there. As you can see in the Table of Contents in the beginning, I've organised these Tips, Techniques and Action Steps for you in subjects for you to deep dive into, if you prefer. Choose from Sales, Networking, Mindset and Maximising Your Year and how to finish strong. This is your book. Read it in whatever order suits you best.

Q1 will be the biggest chunk as you need to have sales superpowers to develop and convert conversations to clients.

Ready? Let's go.

Here's how to write goals that you will feel driven and excited to achieve.

First write down *specifically* what you want to achieve in Q1. There is space to write at the end of this section.

Check...

1. The goal is written as a positive statement and is specific.

   The unconscious mind doesn't hear negative commands.

   So, for example, if you were setting fitness goals, change 'I don't want to be so unfit' (as your unconscious mind doesn't hear negative commands, you're actually telling yourself that you want to be unfit!) write instead 'I want to be fitter' and then you can add in details to make the goal more specific. So add in, 'I want to be able to run 5K in 30 minutes in three months' time'.

Another example to help you state a business goal in the positive, is to write down that you want to invoice £25,000 in each Quarter of the year (or your desired level of income).

Look at your monetary targets that you wrote down in the 'Get Started and Get Organised' section of this book and divide by 4 to get your Quarterly targets.

Whatever number works for you, start there. We all have to start somewhere!

2. What will you gain by achieving your goal in Q1?

3. What resources do you already have to help you achieve this goal? E.g. your phone, laptop, this book, your skills and talents. What else?

4. What extra resources do you need, if any?

5. How will you know you're on track? Each month, make a note of what you have achieved. You can then review monthly, or weekly if you prefer, and adjust your action plan along the way if necessary.

I will give you clear Action Points throughout this book, to keep you on track.

6. When you achieve your goal, is it good for those around you too? Think how this may affect your family, close friends or staff when you have achieved your goal.

7. Consider what will happen if you don't achieve it.

   - What *won't* happen?

   - What will you lose by having this goal? (frustration and stress! what else?)

8. Now imagine you have already achieved your goal.

What will you look like? Create a vivid picture of yourself. What are you doing? What do you see?

What do you hear and what are you saying to yourself?

Feel how you will feel now that you have it. Feels good doesn't it?

9. Allow your learnings from this visualisation to sink in for a few moments.

10. Take a few deep breaths and smile so your brain knows you like it as you create new neural pathways.

The more we do something the easier it gets. Repeat this exercise as often as you like and strengthen those new neural pathways.

Now we're going to deep dive into sales activity so you can tap into your sales superpowers and turn more conversations into paying customers and loyal clients who keep coming back for more, known as *repeat business*.

Sales Strategies for success

First, may I ask you, what are your thoughts about Sales?

I always ask this at the beginning of my workshops. Maybe you like sales or if you shudder at the thought of making sales calls, you're not alone. Many business owners when I first meet them or when they arrive at my workshops have been 'sold to' before in a way that had left a bad feeling.

But it can be done differently.

See how *you* can do this better and help improve your customers' experience, so *they enjoy buying from you.*

What I want to achieve in Q1...

M I T

What's the #1 Most Important Thing I need to do right now, to help me move towards my goal?

MYMM 2. DATE:

BUSTING BELIEFS AND THEN BOOSTING BELIEFS

Remember a time when you have had an amazing experience buying something and you've walked out of the shop, purchase in hand, smiling, or if you've bought a new pair of shoes, suit, or a complete new outfit, feeling ecstatic!

What was the difference? What made that sale such a pleasure to be a *part* of? For me, it's usually when time and attention has been spent on me, the customer, asking me a few questions, finding out what I like, making great suggestions, being genuinely interested.

And you? What made that sale such a pleasure for you?

So why do so many people get turned off from selling?

When I first meet my clients their most common myths are:

1. Sales is scary, so I'd rather not go there!

2. I don't need to sell anything, people know what I do

3. Aaaaggghhh, I can't do it

4. It's not going to work, I'll leave that bit out and go on social media more

5. If I call someone, I'm interrupting them, and bothering someone

6. Even if I do call, they won't want it anyway

7. I won't call, I'll just send another email, it will be OK

8. I don't want to be annoying and keep calling them

9. They have a fear of rejection, or in some people, a fear of success.

10. I haven't got time, I'll do it tomorrow.

Do any of those reasons, or beliefs, sound familiar to you?

What's yours? I want you to write them down on a piece of paper. **Not in this book,** you'll find out why soon. So please get a separate piece of paper.

Write down your beliefs and reasons as to why you don't like sales.

All of them.

Have you done it?

Good.

Now, take one last look at what you've written, quickly scan the list and now screw up the piece of paper, say goodbye to it and throw it in the bin. Yes, that's right throw them away because that's the last time you will see them!

Now, let's change those preconceptions and bust those beliefs.

What if doing more sales activity *does* work?

What if by feeling a little more confident you can achieve what you want to see in your successful business? Then what would happen?

Yes, you'll get more results. You'll be financially independent. You'll be taking control of your business. You'll have a successful business.

First, please promise me you'll do the exercise on the previous page.

Say goodbye to those myths and those fears.

What you fear is generated by your thoughts, and you experience feeling those thoughts. That is all.

When you feel fear, do you feel good? No, I thought not.

Your desires deserve more of your time. You'll feel great if you think about what you desire more. Try it!

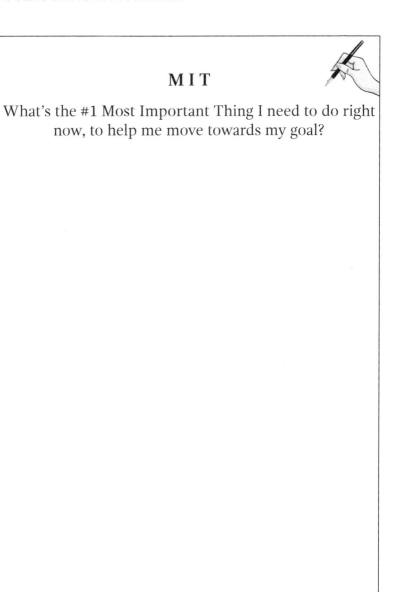

MIT

What's the #1 Most Important Thing I need to do right now, to help me move towards my goal?

MYMM 3.

EXPLODING THE BENEFITS

Step away from the features! Explode the benefits

Have you noticed how sometimes business people talk about the intricacies and minute details of what they *do* but you're still not sure what that *means to you*? Probably because they are talking about the features of their services and products. But don't get caught up just talking about the *features* of your work.

Our clients don't exactly get excited by the features, it's the *benefits* they want! The benefits they will experience after you have designed their website, arranged their event, coached their managers...[enter your expertise here].

Talking about how your clients *benefit* from working with you is a critical part of the sales process. When people see and hear these benefits, they then get excited, happy and pleased their problems will be solved.

You are creating an emotional response and that's when people make the decision to buy.

Learning how to describe what you do using *benefits* instead of features will help you have an easier flowing conversation. You'll be more relaxed and your clients will understand how you can help *them and what it will do for their business and lives*. Talk about the benefits more and you'll win more business.

People buy the benefits of your service or product. They don't buy the features.

So, when you are explaining the features of your service or product, remember to tell them how they will benefit from these.

Also, be careful of jargon that may seem so familiar to you, but we don't understand what you mean.

For example:

As I incorporate 'NLP techniques' into my 'coaching' I used to get excited telling people about this brilliant 'Anchor Technique' or I can do a 'submodality switch'.

Yes, exactly. What am I talking about?! These are all 'features' of what I do. But how does that help you?

We need to talk about how clients will *benefit* from what you do.

For example the *benefits* of a submodality switch allow me to help people free themselves from self-sabotaging beliefs, allowing them to breakthrough what's been holding them back from their success. They can then get on with what they want to do feeling happier and more confident with more helpful beliefs.

I helped two women in the AmberLife Mind Spa recently with this and they're feeling so much better already and as they felt much more confident they accepted the opportunity to speak on stage. This attracted new ideal clients into their world and they won new business quickly afterwards. Amanda, raised a substantial amount of money for the charity she worked with. I'm so proud of them. You'd rather hear about that wouldn't you?

How can you talk about the *benefits* your clients will get from working with you or using the products you provide?

Make a list of some of your *features* and by the side of each one, write out how your clients will *benefit* from these, so you can see them.

Think about how you're going to *help* them and the *results* they will get from working with you.

It's all about the benefits to *them*, not you.

So, your Action Point today is to identify ALL the things you help your clients with.

1. Make a list of ALL the f*eatures* of your services, company and experience.

2. Next to each feature, write down how your clients will *benefit* from them.

    How do the features of your services benefit their lives, improve their business, relationships, health?

There's a template over the page that you can use to help you do this exercise.

Features

Benefits

Explode the benefits

People will connect with you more if you share how using your services and products will benefit them.

Remember: People buy *benefits*, not features. You want to create an emotive response.

Keep looking at the benefits and ask yourself why that is important, five times!

For example, if you are a fitness coach you might ask your prospective client...

"Why is looking after your health important?" And they might answer, *"Because I want to lose weight"*

"Why is losing weight important to you?"
"Because I will be fitter."

"Why is that important to you?"
"Because I will feel good, fit into my jeans and will be able to move around easier.

"Why is moving around easier important to you?"
"So I can actually run again!"

"Why do you want to run again?"
"So I can play football with my children."

Ah, so by probing a little more, by spending more time to discover the trigger for wanting to hire you as a fitness coach, as you can see, the person who wants to get fit, really wants to be able to play football and spend more quality time with his or her children.

I call this exercise, 'exploding the benefits' to discover the ultimate benefit. The real reason someone is going to buy from you. Write your exploded benefits opposite.

Your Action Point is to take some time today to do the above exercise and get crystal clear on your benefits and how you help people.

M I T

What's the #1 Most Important Thing I need to do right now, to help me move towards my goal?

MYMM 4.

STOP UNDERSELLING YOURSELF

How much are you charging for your services or products?

Don't take your skills and expertise for granted. What you might think everyone can do, they probably can't! That's why they need you. They value your skills and experience.

Do you sometimes have limiting beliefs and ask yourself *"how on earth can I charge that much for x, y, z?"*

Now go back to page 72 and look at your list of ALL the things you help your clients with and I bet that question (and limiting belief) fades into the background.

In my experience most small business owners undercharge for their services and products and could easily double the price.

So, now would be a great time to increase the price of your services, wouldn't it?

Where can you double the price of your services? Which ones? Write your answers in the space on the next page.

Where my clients have doubled their prices they have never lost any significant business and only significantly increased their revenues. They raised their game. They felt more confident. They closed (asked for) and won more *profitable* business and ideal clients.

Go and have a look at the list of benefits again and notice how you are improving your customers' lives and business with your services and products.

So, how much are you going to charge for your services and products now?

You can do it. I believe in you.

And when you believe it, your clients will.

Where can I double the price of my services?

M I T

What's the #1 Most Important Thing I need to do right
now, to help me move towards my goal?

YOU

CAN

DO

IT

MYMM 5.

HOW TO PREPARE FOR CLIENT CONVERSATIONS

"Seek first to understand, then to be understood" is the #5 Habit of *Highly Effective People,* by Stephen Covey. He was a renowned author and motivational speaker and inspired millions of people in his life, worldwide.

Most people do not listen with the intent to understand, they listen with the intent to reply. Once you understand more about your client's needs and desires, you will be able to pinpoint the solution that you can provide and tailor it to their needs.

So prepare thoroughly, listen well and allow the conversation to flow and the results will follow.

Spend time finding out what your customer wants first.

This may sound obvious, but how many times have you been sold at or talked at, without being asked any questions as to your preferences, usage, long term plans?

Ask more questions. Listen well.

When you're liaising with your prospects and clients, remember that you will deepen rapport and understanding if you talk only 20% of the conversation and the prospect speaks 80%, you will have the ratios about right. People want to be heard first.

So, your Action Point today is to write out 10 questions to help you have sales conversations with your prospective clients and contacts.

➠ What do you want to know next time you talk to a prospect?

➠ What situation are they in right now?

➠ What do they want to achieve?

➠ What services do they specialise in?

➠ What's important to them?

➠ Do they already use a supplier similar to yours?

➠ What budget do they have?

➠ How can you help?

As you can see there are lots to choose from! What do you really want to know when you are talking to your contacts and having great sales conversations? Write your questions in the table on the opposite page.

Questions when asked in a friendly manner and woven into a conversation, not firing questions off one by one, but asked with genuine interest and care, create useful sales conversations and develop more meaningful relationships. Remember to listen well and take notes.

Find out what your contacts and the person you're talking to need specifically, and you'll find the beginning of the sales process so much more do-able and friendly and the results will follow.

Don't presume the answers. Find out the answers instead, and your customer will feel listened to, cared for and respected. That's the way we like to feel when we buy something, isn't it?

Type up your Top 10 Questions to use as a template to guide you in having better conversations.

Your Top 10 Questions

1	
2	
3	
4	
5	
6	
7	
8	
9	
10	

When people are talking, sometimes they go off on a tangent. Maybe you will, or the person you're talking to will. So by having these questions written down you will be able to focus on what the person is saying, not trying to think of what to ask next. You'll also be able to steer the conversation back round to your objectives if you do go off on a tangent.

Preparing these questions will allow you to be totally present on the call and the results will follow. Listen out for opportunities to ask your customers more questions.

If this feels odd to you at the beginning, relax, as you know, it will feel more natural to you, the more you do it.

**Be more curious, ask more questions
and see more results.**

M I T

What's the #1 Most Important Thing I need to do right
now, to help me move towards my goal?

Who have I met networking that I want to keep in
touch with?

New Leads and Enquiries...

MYMM 6.

CIRCLE OF INFLUENCE — WHO DO YOU KNOW ALREADY?

Who's in your circle of influence?

Have you ever noticed that sometimes the person that can help you the most is right under your nose or already in your circle of influence? Sometimes they're so close we miss them!

It's of course helpful to work out what you'd like help with.

Are you trying to think about everything all by yourself? People are usually happy to help you, if they know *who* you want to be introduced to.

Work out who you want to be introduced to and why.

Making time to connect with your top influencers can really help you build your business. One way is to seek out people that have the same target market as yourself but offer different services.

For example, a divorce lawyer is a top influencer for an IFA, an independent financial advisor. The client will need financial help during and after getting divorced, so the lawyer will recommend their contacts to the IFA which gives a great service to the lawyer's clients as more things are organised for them to help them in their transition. Giving a great complete offering to their clients.

And at the same time the divorce lawyer and the IFA are winning more clients for each other and building their businesses.

It's great to have these people on your side, looking out for you, being an ambassador, creating opportunities and introductions to your ideal clients, being a part of your team. It feels good working together.

Your Action Point today is to take some time to identify who are key influencers in your circle.

I bet you know them already. So, schedule some time to get to know them better and develop the relationships. Through trust and understanding more business opportunities will appear.

Key influencers in my circle...

Make a point of meeting with these influencers regularly, either at networking events, or on a one-to-one basis.

And of course return the favour. Who can you help? How will you reach out to them?

Today I want to give you a nudge to use one of your beloved gadgets, in a different way to help you develop your relationships and achieve the results you want to see in your business.

And I'm going to start with some facts. Not just from me, from my clients too.

Fact Number 1.
There are '4 words' to help you grow your business, they are...

Pick Up The Phone

Fact Number 2.
It works a treat! Here's how...

Two weeks ago, my client, Victoria, sat down at her desk, figured out what revenue she needed to generate that month, and decided who to call. And brilliant, after picking up the phone that day, to only 8 contacts, she generated **extra business** of **£8,150,** so this means...

> FACT
> Every time she picked up the phone,
> in one day, she earned £1,018.75

Another client, Claire, who felt motivated by this news when I told her about Victoria's results, picked up the phone to her 9 prospects and secured an **extra £4,500** that day.

> FACT
> Every time she picked up the phone,
> she earned £500.

Plus during the calls she also arranged 3 client meetings with her prospects. So, the opportunities are there to increase this amount after she's attended her meetings.

So don't be shy of the phone, look at it with love. Your phone is your #1 money making device!

How much would you like to earn **every time** you pick up the phone? £500? £1,000? £2,000?

Fact Number 3.

Not everyone is going to say yes, right there and then, BUT...

My clients told me these 5 results they have gained from picking up the phone.

1. You can understand your client's needs, fears and desires so much quicker when you talk to them, as opposed to just emailing them.

2. You can get your passion across, using your voice, more easily, than in an email. And importantly, you can hear *their* voice and response.

3. You can get feedback on your proposal quicker.

4. You can answer any questions your clients and prospects may have during the call, which is much faster than emailing each other throughout the coming weeks.

5. You can hear "Yes please, I'd like to go ahead and work with you", more often. Imagine how good that will feel.

My clients have noticed that the more they *pick up the phone* the more their fears around it have dissipated.

➤ Practise ◄
➤ By doing it ◄

Like most things we fear, when we've done it, we realise we're still standing! We're still alive! This boost to your neural pathways creates those feel-good grooves, which helps you perform even better, when we do it next time.

PLUS: My clients told me *no one* was rude to them when they called them!

No one said, "please don't call me ever again!" and

No one said, "what a cheek you have calling me!"

My clients are now loving their phones, and not just for the apps and social media!

So, who are you going to call? Let's find out on Monday.

MIT

What's the #1 Most Important Thing I need to do right now, to help me move towards my goal?

Who have I met networking that I want to keep in touch with?

New Leads and Enquiries...

WHO'S YOUR TOP 10?

I invite you to take 15 minutes this morning to have a look at your prospect and client list (including that pile of business cards on your desk or still in your bag that are yet to go on your excel spreadsheet, in your contacts, your CRM or your own database).

Select 10 people that you would love to do business with.

It's time to get back in your driving seat, go up a gear and start making sales. You know you want to. Sales isn't scary, sales is all about relationships. It's a P2P world – people buy from people.

Pick out 10 businesses that you would love to work with.

➡ Who can you help?

➡ Who are your ideal clients?

➡ You have your list of benefits to review from page 72. Who would love to receive them?

➡ Who have you met recently that you had a good connection with?

➡ Who have you identified that you would *love* to work with?

Put them on your Top 10. I have included a list of examples on the next page to help you identify your Top 10.

Examples of who to put on your Top 10:

1. Who have you met recently who you would like to work with ?

2. Your Influencers

3. People you met networking

4. Existing clients – catch up, quarterly review

5. Referrals you've gained

6. People from Social Media you want to meet

7. People you've sent proposals to

8. Specific companies you are targeting

9. Someone from last month you need to follow up with again

10. Ideal Clients from the leads and enquiries you've gained.

Put them on your Top 10 and give them a call. They might not need you right now, but you will start creating your sales cycle and importantly, you will start to develop the relationship. Put a time in your diary to call them again, in 3, 6 or 9 months' time.

Your Action Point today is to identify your Top 10. Select your Top 10 to work on this month. Set your intention. Things happen after you do!

Treat yourself to a wipe board and hang it in your office where you can see it to remind you who your Top 10 are.

You can use the template on page 94 to get started.

Your Top 10 is THE #1 most important element of your business development which you need to take action on every month if you want to grow your business and see great results.

Having a minimum of 10 conversations with potential clients each month, with your network and businesses you would love to work with, will definitely improve your results and you'll make more sales.

My clients love this. The Top 10 template could earn you £100,000 this year and more. Yes it can!

Depending on how much you are charging for your services and products, and how fast you are converting your leads and enquiries, you may need to increase your Top 10 to a Top 20, or Top 50, etc.

It's better to do more business development activity in the first instance so you can make more headway on your goals. By talking to more decision makers about your business and how you can help them, you will double your chances of success.

You will be able to monitor your performance too, and can then tweak it for even more results.

For optimum results you need to make 10 calls in a month with decision makers. You will have skills within this book to help you convert some conversations into clients over the phone. You will also grow your business faster if you attend a minimum of 3 meetings in a month too. You need to scale this for what your business and sales targets require.

If in a typical month, from your Top 10 you convert 3 conversations or meetings into new paying clients, you then have data to work with.

From knowing this information, if you want to double your sales, then double your activity. For example, if you want 6 pieces of business next month, you need to make 20 calls and have a minimum of 6 meetings to convert your activity into 6 sales. Work out how much each conversion is worth and you'll start to realise your efforts and how important picking up the phone is and meeting prospects on a regular basis.

My clients are always surprised when they first start doing this as their clients are thrilled to hear from them. They're happy they called. They acquire new clients.

What's not to like?

So, go ahead and identify your Top 10 prospects and people from your network who you would like to start developing a relationship with and find out more about them and their business.

Make your Mondays matter and work your Top 10.

My Top 10

1.

2.

3.

4.

5.

6.

7.

8.

9.

10.

My 3 Meetings this month

Date:

Name:

Contact details:

Location or online:

Any other info:

Date:

Name:

Contact details:

Location or online:

Any other info:

Date:

Name:

Contact details:

Location or online:

Any other info:

MIT

What's the #1 Most Important Thing I need to do right now, to help me move towards my goal?

Who have I met networking that I want to keep in touch with?

New Leads and Enquiries...

MYMM 8.

STAND OUT FROM THE CROWD TODAY
AND MAKE MORE SALES

Well done, you've got your Top 10 List of Prospects now.

Doesn't that feel good to have more clarity and focus on who you'll be working with?

When was the last time you spoke to one of them?

We love a quick text here and an Instagram post there. Social media is great but taking the time to call someone as well, really does make a big difference to your results.

A phone call.

Remember those 4 little words that will mean so much success to you: *Pick up the phone!*

I encourage you to pick up the phone now and call one of your Top 10.

Did you just say you don't like making sales calls? Sales calls aren't scary. Remember, sales is all about relationships. By calling someone you're simply connecting and chatting. Your ideal customers are probably sitting in their office right now, just like you and would really welcome a good chat about their business. You will learn more about them and you could make someone's day.

So, your Action Point today is to *Pick up the phone!*

Set a goal to talk to 3 of your contacts today. Do more if you want to. If they're in, chat, if they sound busy when they answer, ask them if this is a good time to talk and if not, ask what time would be better tomorrow, and put it in your diary.

Have a look at your Top 10 Questions that you have already prepared.

Also, ask your contact what they need to help them with their business now or in the near future. If you can do it, then great, you will have a new client to start working with.

If you can't help them, I bet you know someone who can. Recommend someone in your network and you have become a good resource for your contacts. They will remember you for it.

Ask your prospective clients what they've been doing since the last time you saw them, what projects are they working on, Ask them, "what help do you need?" Listen carefully, I love that word, carefully = full of care.

Listen carefully and record the new information into your CRM, your database or Excel sheet of clients and prospects, wherever you are storing your client and prospect information to be able to refer to during future conversations.

Pick up the phone! You can do it.

Make your Mondays matter now!

Top telephone tips that will improve your sales conversions

Are you taking the time to call people but not getting the results you want?

If you're finding it hard to get hold of people, discover how you can boost your sales with these **3 tweaks to make your sales calls more productive.**

1. **When is the best time to call?** – one lady set aside some time each day at 11am to call people, but kept getting their voicemail. So, I suggest, try different times. Many of your contacts will be doing their client work between 10am and midday and between 2pm and 4pm.

    So, change the time you call. Do you know if they are a morning person? You could call at 8.30am to 9.30am, before they get stuck into their day. It's good to call between 12 and 2pm during lunch break or after 4pm. Try different times and you'll see when works best.

2. **Do they sound busy?** Importantly, listen out for their tone of voice and notice if they sound relaxed and happy to talk, or did they sound rushed when they answered the phone? If rushed, arrange a more suitable time to talk. It's OK. Don't feel pressured you have to talk to them that minute. It's good manners to ask, isn't it.

3. **Did you go through to their voicemail?** If you know them, leave a message asking them to call you back. You could also write a brief email saying "I called to catch up, are you free later on today or tomorrow morning please?" If you don't know them very well, I wouldn't leave a voicemail. Just call them back at a different time.

Advanced selling skills for you

How to Mirror elegantly to Make More Sales

As selling is a vital skill to learn to grow your business, and happily stay in business, today, I'm going to give you a new superpower to help you build *and stay* in rapport, with ease.

You've heard of mirroring body language, how it helps build rapport?

The person sitting in front of you crosses their legs, so you cross yours. You then notice they have shifted their body to sit more prominently on their right side, so you shift yours, sitting more on your left, to 'mirror' their body language.

Done well, it's a good technique to help you build rapport with 'non-verbal' cues. Being a sales trainer, it was obvious to me if an experienced sales person was using the technique on me, it was a great game, as I scratched the left side of my head, and they did the same. I crossed my left leg, he crossed his right. But done too quickly, it's obvious. If you are going to do it, slow down, as you mirror their movements. Not every movement, as it's so obvious!

It works when you're in meetings, but it doesn't work over the phone as you can't see them. So, what do you do in this situation? How can you build rapport when you can't see them?

Here's how you can build rapport elegantly when talking on the phone.

Notice what language they are using when they describe different experiences.

Are they using more visual/auditory/kinæsthetic terms when they give you an objection? For example, they might say, "Ah, I can't really *see* how that will help us right now." Or they may say, they need to *hear* it again and talk it through before a decision can be made. Or they *feel* uncomfortable with the price and need to know more.

Listen to determine your client's preferred system of language. They'll usually use their preferred system during the conversation.

The three main preferred systems are:

Visual = See

Auditory = Hear

Kinæsthetic = Feel

Discovering the words they use to express themselves, gives vital information. It's not a personality test and doesn't reveal anything more than knowing what their preferred system of language is when they remember, recall and recount experiences. But this vital insight will help you stay in rapport and develop rapport as you *mirror* their *language*.

As you listen to them speak, and I mean, really listen to the words they are using, how they describe what they like (kinaesthetic) about their current supplier, or what they are looking (visual) for in their next training partner, or the way your proposal sounds (auditory).

Listen carefully and notice the words they use, so you can elegantly use the same preferred system – visual, auditory or kinaesthetic, and mirror their language. Because it works.

It works when you are in meetings and presentations too and allows you to build rapport with everyone in the room as you express yourself, talk about your services and products using the three main systems during the meeting, addressing each attendee using their preferred system.

Have a go today.

Your Action Point is to purposefully and carefully listen to your client's words, and every so often, especially as you close for the next step, speak the same language.

Weave in those Visual, Auditory or Kinæsthetic words your customer speaks, and deepen rapport. I call this element in my Advanced Sales Training course, 'Talk a Deeper Talk' and when done elegantly it is a wonderful way to let your customers know you understand them, which leads to more sales.

Mirror their tempo at first too.

Slow your speed down, if they talk slowly, or they might not catch what you're saying.

Speed up, if they talk quickly, or they might get impatient!

Mirror first to build rapport, then adjust to your way of talking a few minutes into the conversation. Mirror, pace and lead, as we call it in Sales Training.

Look at your Top 10. Pick up the phone to your contacts and arrange those meetings.

If you secured 3 new business opportunities this month, what would that be worth financially to you?

I can imagine your new sales skills are being put into practice. Good work.

Preparation, preparation, preparation

Recently I helped one of my clients, Valerie, prepare her presentation for a 12-month multiple 6-figure contract. I was so impressed by how much time she had taken to answer questions and probable objectives her client might ask her. She also prepared for and demonstrated in her presentation a satisfied customer scenario, *as if she was already hired*. Brilliant.

Yes it took time, *extra* time, but she felt so confident in the meeting, the stress dissipated. And she sparkled and won the contract.

How much time do you take to prepare for your meetings or business presentations?

How much time do you take to prepare before you make that important phone call?

Preparation is your friend.
Preparation creates excellence.

Yes you might think that you can wing it. And maybe you can, but I bet you will get even better results if you *are* more prepared.

Each time you are with someone, whether in person or over the phone, online or offline, you only have a certain amount of time to **connect, engage and influence**.

Don't waste that time or opportunity. You might not get a second chance.

Take that *extra* time to prepare and notice the difference it makes.

TOP SALES TIP

Importantly, at the end of each call/presentation, make sure you know, or ask, what will be the next step you and your client will take. When will you talk again to discuss the proposal? When will you meet again to discuss how you can help them?

Don't leave the meeting or end the call without this important piece of information.

Otherwise the client may feel confused as to what is going to happen next, or worse case, think you're not interested in working with them!

MIT

What's the #1 Most Important Thing I need to do right now, to help me move towards my goal?

Who have I met networking that I want to keep in touch with?

New Leads and Enquiries...

MYMM 9.

PREPARE FOR YOUR MEETINGS WITH YOUR NETWORK.
PLAN AHEAD

Your Action Point today is to prepare more for your client meetings and people you've met networking.

What will you talk about when you meet?

Relax and read on. Choose one of your Top 10.

First have a look at their website; check out news feeds, read their blog, latest PR, videos, social media presence. Familiarise yourself with their business again and pick something you'd like to discuss with them. This demonstrates you are really interested in *them*.

Here are my **Top 5 Questions** for your meeting:

1. **What made you start your business?** Find out what excites them, rekindle their passion for starting their business and learn about their journey. As you may be aware sometimes when you're stressed or haven't got enough time, some people forget why they started it in the first place!

   What's your reason for starting *your* business?

   What's *your* purpose? Prepare answers for this question too.

2. **Who do you generally work with?** Find out their target market, as you may have a contact

who would love to meet them too. Is there any synergy in what you both do?

3. **What project are you working on?** If they are having a problem, can your services or products solve that for them? Tell them how.

4. **What's the one thing you need now to help you?** A virtual assistant? A new accountant? A coach?

5. **Who would be a good contact for you to meet?** Think of your network and do some matchmaking, it helps the world go round. Who would be a good contact for you too? They will probably ask you, so be prepared.

These questions will really help you to get to know your contacts more and find out how you can help them directly or by introducing someone else you know.

Enjoy your meetings. Prepare first for best results.

My powerful top tip is to *imagine the meeting going really well.* See yourself smiling and enjoying the experience, hear yourself answering questions with ease, being passionate, informative, helpful...you get the picture! Notice how good you are feeling now as you imagine your meeting working out brilliantly.

Now I am going to share my top tip to quickly build rapport at meetings with people you don't know very well. This tip also works if you are meeting the decision maker for the first time.

If you are going to a meeting at someone's offices for the first time, have a look online or call ahead and find out what the general dress code is so that you can reflect them and their company culture, already. Look like you fit in with them and you are already sending positive signals to the team or the decision maker that you understand them, you have common goals and interests. If they're suited, arrive suited too. If they're in jeans or dress-down, then smart casual is a good option.

Remember you never get a second chance to make a first impression.

Recall the time you made a good first impression.

Think about what you were wearing when you had success and felt great or imagine exactly what that *will* feel like.

Remember a time ...

➠ When you won your last piece of business
➠ When you felt super-confident as you left your office and went to a meeting
➠ When you felt at your most comfortable AND confident
➠ When you received a compliment when out at a networking event.

What were you wearing? It obviously suited you and helped you to start building rapport as you had made a good first impression, well done. Wear it again, or something similar that makes you feel good.

MIT

What's the #1 Most Important Thing I need to do right now, to help me move towards my goal?

Who have I met networking that I want to keep in touch with?

New Leads and Enquiries...

MYMM 10.

NURTURING YOUR RELATIONSHIPS

Only 1% of sales happen on the first point of contact.

So... you need to nurture your relationships in your network online and offline to help you make more sales.

"How often should I follow up?" people ask me.

After you've attended a networking event, do you follow up with your connections more than once?

What will happen if you follow up more?

Good news!

Here are some stats to encourage you to follow up and carry on the conversation...

[1]**80% of sales are made on the 5th to 12th contact.**

So, you need to take the time to build relationships with your prospects, ideal clients and network to create more opportunities and the results will follow.

More shocking stats....

[2]**Only about 50% of people even follow up once,**

25% follow up twice

and only 12% follow up 3 times.

---

1. McGrath Hill Research
2. McGrath Hill Research

So, be different and take the initiative to follow up more. You *will* make more sales this way.

Who have you just thought of getting in touch with again?

Give them a call and have a chat. I'm sure they'll be delighted to hear from you.

A question I get asked many times by my clients and which is always a point of conversation during my workshops, is "won't I be interrupting them?"

There's always the worry that you're hassling people, interrupting their day and of course, you might be!

But if you don't follow up with the contacts that you have already made, you may be missing out on opportunities to develop the relationship further. And sales is all about relationships.

Identify people to follow up with, again.

Who did you call or meet up with a few months ago and have not spoken to since?

Follow Up today and call them.

Remember those stats, 'Only about 50% of people even follow up once, 25% follow up twice and only 12% follow up three times.'

Follow up more and you will make more sales.

Your Action Point today is to write down 3 people you need to follow up with today, or refer to your Top 10 and call them.

Let's go!

M I T

What's the #1 Most Important Thing I need to do right now, to help me move towards my goal?

Who have I met networking that I want to keep in touch with?

New Leads and Enquiries...

MYMM II.

WAYS YOU CAN DIG DEEPER
TO MAKE MORE SALES

Do you find you're sometimes lost for words when your prospective customer says something like 'oh, you're too expensive'? Or, 'I'm talking to a few suppliers, I'll get back to you'?

Don't shy away at this point. Take a breath and ask more questions. You just need to know more about your customers' needs before they buy.

Here are some questions to help you gather more information during your sales conversations – to dig a little deeper – to help you understand your customers better, helping you to close more business.

So, let's look at 3 ways that you can dig deeper and gather the information they haven't told you, yet!

1. **If it's a pricing query you're stuck on**

    If they say 'you're too expensive', ask them, "compared to who?" or "compared with what?"

    Just like we all shop in different supermarkets – you can find out what kind of supplier they are looking for. The cheapest, mid-range, or a higher quality service?

2. **If it's a service level query you're stuck on**

    If they say, "I'm talking to other suppliers", ask them "What do you like about their service or the product they are offering?"

    or, "What's missing from their service that you'd like to have so you're confident you're getting the best fit for your business needs?"

    or "what are you looking for specifically, so you're confident you're getting the best service for your business needs, budget and goals?"

3. **If it's a values-driven query you're stuck on**

    One of my favourite questions that uncovers your customers' main drivers is:

    "What's the most important thing about [insert their need here]?"

Their answers will tell you exactly how you need to demonstrate where you can add value to their business or lifestyle and how you can help them.

So today, your Action Point is to dig deeper when you're talking with your customers and clients.

Don't presume the answers.

Find out the answers instead, and your customer will feel listened to, cared for and respected. And that's the way we like to feel when we buy something, isn't it?

Make your Mondays matter, dig deep!

Discover your Customer's Buying Journey

Are you ready to convert more leads that have come in through your website, referrals and networking recommendations?

Are you ready to 'close' and ask for the business during your sales conversations?

OK, I hear you, you feel funny when it gets to the 'closing' part, you 'hate this bit', or worse, you 'forget to say this bit!' or, you 'don't like asking for money?'

You're not alone. It's OK. I'm here to help. Do you want to help more customers?

Here's a brilliant question to help you define if your customers are ready to work with you. Or if they are ready to 'close' themselves!

Let's find out where your customers are on their buying journey.

⥤ You've prepared for your phone calls, meetings and have your Top 10 Questions ready for your conversations.
⥤ You've picked up the phone and talked to your prospective customers and had good conversations!
⥤ You know how often it's good to follow up now don't you?
⥤ You know the value of what your customers gain from working with you.

Excellent.

So, now, ask the question to determine where your customers are on their buying journey....

"How long have you been thinking about doing this?"

This will help you determine if they have just thought about it, and are maybe only in the research phase or if they've been thinking about it for a couple of months and are still looking for the right person and solution to help them. Or it could be that they're at the 6-month stage and have finally had enough of their situation!

Listen carefully to what they say.

Most people can only put up with things for so long, and 6 months is about it. So if relevant, ask them, again...

"For how much longer can you put up with this situation?"

If they are stuck and want to get out of the situation they are in now, they will tell you the answer and 'close' themselves.

So ask them, "Are you ready to go ahead now or do you need more information from me?" Another great 'closing question' so you can see where your client is on their journey. Read the Action Point in the next section too as this will explain THE best closing question ever, and it's easy to use and very, very effective.

Have a go. Go on! I'm cheering you on from here. What's the worst that could happen? You'll still be in the same boat, right?

What's the best that can happen....... ?

........Exactly!

MIT

What's the #1 Most Important Thing I need to do right
   now, to help me move towards my goal?

Who have I met networking that I want to keep in
   touch with?

New Leads and Enquiries...

My Top 10

1.

2.

3.

4.

5.

6.

7.

8.

9.

10.

My 3 Meetings this month

Date:

Name:

Contact details:

Location or online:

Any other info:

Date:

Name:

Contact details:

Location or online:

Any other info:

Date:

Name:

Contact details:

Location or online:

Any other info:

MYMM 12.

INTRODUCING THE BEST CLOSING TECHNIQUE EVER!

There are many closing techniques you can use to help you close for the next step or close for the business. 'Closing' is a term used in sales to describe techniques and situations to help you make progress and win new business.

You can 'close' for the next step. For example, using one of the techniques you'll discover here in this chapter, you will help your prospects and clients to decide when they are available to discuss your proposal, or will start working with you, or how much in volume of a product they want to buy.

You can also 'close' for the business. This is using one of the techniques to win the business.

Here are 3 'closing' techniques you can use.

1. **The Presumptive Close** – when you assume your contact has everything they need and are going to work with you.

   During the conversation, you say "Let's start on Tuesday" which "presumes" they want to go ahead and Tuesday works for them too.

2. **The 'Sense of Urgency' close** – for example, a specific timed offer or a limited number of people you work with each month prompts the person to make a decision, so they don't miss out.

It's a well-known fact people don't want to miss out on something, or FOMO, (Fear Of Missing Out) as it's often called, so it's a good driver to help people make a decision.

3. **The Alternative Close** – This is THE most effective 'close'.

   When you use the Alternative Close, you are giving people a choice by offering them an alternative that still works for you too. A choice.

   Offer your client, A or B.

   If A or B doesn't suit them, they will tell you C. This way they feel in control and they have made the decision themselves, which they have, and so are comfortable with continuing to work with you, or buy your product.

   This is my favourite technique that I use, and my clients use and love it, to great effect.

   This is by far, THE best closing technique I have ever discovered, and my clients use it ALL the time. Because it works. Use it in your emails too.

Here are some examples of how you can use The Alternative Close

"Would you like to meet up on Tuesday or Thursday, which is best for you?"

This certainly helps people to make a decision when they look in their busy diaries.

You're offering two dates. If they're not free on either of those dates, (A or B) they will suggest when they are (C). It works a treat!

"Are you ready to go ahead now we've talked or would you like to meet up before you make your decision?"

You are helping to develop the relationship and take it to the next stage.

"These are the two options that by working together will give you the results you are looking for. Option A is ....or Option B is ...... I recommend A. What's your preference?"

You are advising them which will work best for them and they are in the position of making the decision themselves.

"Great, thank you for your business, I look forward to working with you. To process the invoice, if I could please take your details. (Ask them for company name and address) *Thank you. Would you like to pay by bank transfer or via PayPal?"*

Giving them the choice of how they prefer to pay.

If they are not yet in a position to buy and ask for more information, say...

"Sure, thanks for your time, I'll send you the information we've discussed. When's good to catch up for your feedback? Tomorrow afternoon or Friday morning?"

Always ask when you can speak to them again.

This way you'll know, so you don't play the waiting game, or feel unsure as to when to phone them back. Don't leave things hanging.

Ask, giving them the Alternative Close.

People get overwhelmed with too many options and people like to feel they are in control, and have a choice.

When people feel they have a choice, they don't feel pressured and a decision comes easier.

My clients always tell me how well it works for them, how it's so much easier to arrange meetings, calls and closing for the business.

And importantly, they tell me how *good* they feel doing it.

This is key to gaining new meetings with your prospects and clients.

It works with your partner, friends and children too. Practise with them first. For example, I love to cook after work and often ask my husband, "What would you like for dinner? Chicken curry or fish and vegetables?" A or B. He'll answer A or B, or give me his suggestion, his favourite – Lasagne! Or "Would you like the stew that's left over from yesterday or shall we go out for dinner tonight?" I love that one! A or B. Try it, it's quite fun and gets great results.

Your Action Point today is to work out 3 Alternative Closes for your business. Write them down below.

My 3 Alternative Closes...

1.

2.

3.

By adding sales activity consistently into your schedule will definitely enable you to make more sales. You will be able to convert leads and enquiries you gain from your networking, social media and marketing efforts.

Stop and Eat the Carrots

Wow, you've nearly finished Quarter 1. So I encourage you to take a look and see what you've already achieved in Q1 especially if you made changes. What differences have they made to you and your business so far?

It's extremely important to acknowledge how far you've come. We all get tired if we just keep *chasing* goals.

It's time to stop and eat the carrots!

When working with a client recently, and many of us do this, I noticed at no point did she stop and appreciate all the hard work she was doing, she just kept looking to the next thing, and the next thing. No wonder she was feeling worn out and slightly frustrated with running her business. If you feel like this, stop a moment. Breathe.

Don't just dangle carrots (or goals) in front of you, and yet never take the time to eat them! Yes goals are great to steer us in the right direction, but if you are always continuously aiming for them, then as you achieve them, you immediately go on to the next without a second thought, you're stopping yourself *from truly appreciating your expertise, and the results you have achieved.*

Today, take time to eat some carrots! Appreciate what you have achieved.

Don't burn yourself out always running to the next thing, before you've stopped to reflect on what you have done.

"Well done" from me, "You're doing great"

Encouragement goes a long way and creates a positive feedback loop.

Sometimes it's not easy is it? Some days are harder than others.

Be kind to yourself.

Stop and say thank you, out loud, to yourself. You're doing really well.

What are you thankful for?

It could be one or many things; be thankful for the small steps you take each day to build your business; be thankful for how you step outside your comfort zone on a regular basis to grow your business, and I bet you have a big list of other things you're thankful for don't you?

As you connect with your *why* and thank yourself, you'll send positive signals to your brain, connect neural pathways that will empower you and encourage you in ways you might not yet have discovered.

Write down what you are thankful for. You can use the space on the next page.

Then, say them out loud. Notice what you notice, as you do. It doesn't matter if someone's listening, they'll be inspired. And if no one's with you right now as you're reading this, well, there is one person who is listening, YOU. Go for it.

I am thankful for...

MIT

What's the #1 Most Important Thing I need to do right now, to help me move towards my goal?

Who have I met networking that I want to keep in touch with?

New Leads and Enquiries...

MYMM 13.

YOUR Q1 ACHIEVEMENT LIST

Today I invite you to write down what you have achieved in Q1. There is space to do this at the end of this section.

Here are some questions to get you started...

1. **What projects have you started and how far have you got with them?** Be honest with your account of your progress. It will truly help you gauge when you'll be able to finish them. Things usually take longer than expected when creating something new, so it's good to see what you've achieved so far. Then re-adjust and set new time frames to finish them.

2. **What was the one thing that you feared before, but now you've done it and overcome your fear?** Always a major achievement in my book – doing something that scared you. It's huge! Well done, treat yourself for doing it.

3. **What has been your biggest improvement in the WAY you work?** What changes did you make? Did you schedule your time differently to achieve more in your day?

4. **What does your revenue look like?** After giving yourself a push in the last few weeks, how do your results compare to the targets you set for Q1?

5. **What offline and online activities gave you more leads and enquiries?** This will help you define where you spend your time in Q2. You can reflect on your popular posts, what subject headers gave you the highest open rates? Check your progress with prospects you have started to connect with. See what results and new contacts you made at your networking events.

6. **What are you *most* pleased to have achieved?**

   Whether you think they are main achievements or small things you have done to get closer to your goals, each step matters, they all count. Recognise them. They are important to you. Value your actions. Your ability. Your efforts. Your wins. Your learnings.

Top Tip

Get into the habit of recognising what you've achieved more often.

Writing an 'Achievement List' at the end of the day or week is a great motivator and it makes a pleasant change to see what you have achieved rather than what's still left to do. And please do treat yourself for working so hard. You deserve it!

Yes, you've completed Q1 and gained your sales superpowers.

To your success and happiness, time to celebrate. Enjoy!

M I T

What's the #1 Most Important Thing I need to do right now, to help me move towards my goal?

Who have I met networking that I want to keep in touch with?

New Leads and Enquiries...

My Achievements in Q1

1.

2.

3.

4.

5.

6.

Well done from me, you rock!

QUARTER 2

MAKE YOUR NETWORKING MATTER
AND Q2 GOALS

MYMM 14.

TAKE TIME TO REFLECT ON Q1
— HOW DID YOU GET ON?

First off let's look at your figures and take some time to reflect on what happened in Q1 before you set your goals for Q2.

> **REMEMBER**
> the AmberLife #1 Business Growth Rule is
> **"Repeat what works, tweak what's not, or ditch it"**

Let's start.

⟹ Take some time to check your figures for Q1, January to March. How did you get on? Did you hit your targets and goals? Can you see what you can repeat or tweak to help you improve even more?

⟹ What do you need to do to make Q2 work well for you?

⟹ What do you need to repeat?

⟹ What do you need to tweak?

⟹ What do you need to ditch?

With the knowledge gained from the data you collected from your results in Q1 and by reflecting, you are now in a position to set your Goals for Q2.

What I want to achieve in Q2...

First write down *specifically* what you want to achieve in Q2. You can do that in the space opposite.

Check...

1. The goal is written as a positive statement and is specific.

   Remember, your unconscious mind doesn't hear negative commands.

2. To help you state a business goal in the positive, write down your monetary goal with the date of the last day of the Quarter. For example, you want to generate business to invoice £25,000 by the end of Q2, 30th June.

   What's your monetary target this Quarter? Write it here.

   My monetary target is...

   ---

3. What will you gain by achieving this in Q2?

4. What resources do you already have to help you achieve this goal?

   E.g. your sales superpowers, your Top 10 Questions, your new empowering beliefs. What else?

5. What extra resources do you need? To meet more like-minded people? I've got your back, read on!

6. Are you totally responsible for achieving this goal?

7. When you achieve your goal, is it good for people close to you too?

8. Consider what will happen if you don't achieve your goal.

   ⟹ What won't happen?

   ⟹ What will you lose by having this goal? (Perhaps frustration and stress. What else?)

9. Now fast forward in your mind to the end of Q2 and imagine you have already achieved your goal.

   ⟹ What are you doing?

   ⟹ What do you see?

   ⟹ What do you hear?

   ⟹ What are you saying to yourself?

   ⟹ Feel how you will feel now that you have achieved it. Feels good, doesn't it?

   ⟹ What did you learn or notice?

10. Allow all this new information to sink in for a few moments.

   Take a few deep breaths and smile so your brain knows you like it!

I hope you are becoming more at ease with setting goals and doing this visualisation technique. Repeat steps 9 and 10 as often as you like and strengthen those new neural pathways. They'll look out for you!

MIT

What's the #1 Most Important Thing I need to do right now, to help me move towards my goal?

Who have I met networking that I want to keep in touch with?

New Leads and Enquiries...

MYMM 15.

DATE:

IT'S TIME TO START NETWORKING.

I can imagine that you'd like to work with more clients, yes? Then it's time to start networking.

Why? Networking is one of THE best ways to meet your ideal clients, people who can help you *find* your ideal clients or *recommend* you to their friends, colleagues and contacts, plus you'll meet your peers and other like-minded business owners which is one of the best reasons to go in the first place. You might have to visit a few events before you find the right one for you, but the time you invest in face-to-face networking will be worth it.

Listen well to the person in front of you and maintain good eye contact.

Ask a few questions, engage with them and be genuinely interested in them.

If you're nervous or feeling shy, then focusing on the person in front of you and really listening to what they are saying will help you to forget about yourself!

Your internal dialogue will soften as you focus on the person in front of you and listen to them instead.

If you see someone else looking like they'd rather run out the door, then go and talk to them. They'll be so pleased you did and it will boost your confidence in return.

The best part about people meeting you, is that they get to meet YOU.

Be yourself, that's who they want to meet.

Remember, you are enough.

If you don't have a website yet, networking will still work wonders to help you build your business. You are more than your website.

Josie, one of my clients who had just started her business didn't have a website, but through attending local networking events met 3 people who helped introduce her to top schools in the area where she then went on to secure 2 new pieces of business, delivering mindfulness courses to teachers. All without a website!

Have fun and people will enjoy meeting YOU.

You'll find that people want to meet up for coffee, lunch or have a good chat over the phone with you, to find out more about you.

If you are a seasoned networker already, check that you are doing *all* the following top tips? See if there are one or two points you can improve on.

Here we go. To your business networking success.

M I T

What's the #1 Most Important Thing I need to do right now, to help me move towards my goal?

Who have I met networking that I want to keep in touch with?

New Leads and Enquiries...

My Top 10

1.

2.

3.

4.

5.

6.

7.

8.

9.

10.

My 3 Meetings this month

Date:

Name:

Contact details:

Location or online:

Any other info:

Date:

Name:

Contact details:

Location or online:

Any other info:

Date:

Name:

Contact details:

Location or online:

Any other info:

MYMM 16

PREPARE A MEMORABLE INTRODUCTION
TO MAKE AN IMPACT

When people ask you "What do you do?" Don't just tell them your job title, be different. Make an impact. The person in front of you needs to know *how you help your clients*.

For example, I could say, "I'm Jo, a business coach". But it doesn't tell them much! That's just my name and job title.

Instead I say, "I'm Jo James. I work with business owners who want clarity in *how* they can make more money and grow their business. My clients get REAL results, fast!"

or an even shorter introduction:

"Hi, I'm Jo James, I work with people who want to make more money from their talents and skills and build their business to 6-figures and beyond."

These two opening introductions always pique people's interest to find out more. And so the conversation begins.

Your Action Point today is to prepare your (short) memorable introduction to make an impact. Use the space on the next page to write it down.

Hi, I'm .... from .... I work with ....
who .... (pain point) and want to achieve
................(results).

My short memorable introduction...

Great! I can imagine your introduction is good and will make an impact. This will help you strike up interest and stand out from the crowd because you're able to sum up *quickly* how you help people. This all helps build rapport and the person in front of you is interested in talking to you more so they'll probably start asking you questions. Fantastic!

MIT

What's the #1 Most Important Thing I need to do right now, to help me move towards my goal?

Who have I met networking that I want to keep in touch with?

New Leads and Enquiries...

MYMM 17.

RESEARCH NETWORKING EVENTS AND CLUBS.
WHICH ENVIRONMENT SUITS YOU?

Do you like a mixed environment to socialise over a glass of champagne or a cocktail when networking? Or would you prefer an early breakfast meeting where everyone gets to introduce their own business round the table?

Or would you enjoy a more relaxed lunch event? Or an industry specific event? An evening event with wine? Yes, networking events do seem to circle around food and alcohol, but not all!

Your Action Point today is to book onto a Networking Event.

There are many to choose from, so research and see which one suits you best. Have a look on Eventbrite and similar platforms, type your location into the search bar and see what events are in your area.

Top Tip: If you receive a guest list prior to the event:

➠ Check out some of the guests' websites and pick out a few people who you would like to be introduced to.

➠ When you're researching the guests' websites, what appeals to you? Read one of their blog posts, watch their videos, read about their new hires or news.

➠ When you meet the person it will be easy to start up a conversation as you can compliment them on their website, blog, video, news etc.

➠ Imagine how you'd feel if someone complimented you on your blog or video? Yes that's right, pleased I imagine!

So, take some time to research before you go, and choose something to talk about.

If you are in London or can travel to London, come to my event! It's called Contacts & Cocktails, held monthly near Piccadilly Circus in Central London.

Visit my website at http://www.amberlife.com/london-networking-contacts-cocktails/ to book your ticket and come and say hello. I'd love to meet you and introduce you and your expertise to the other like-minded brilliant business owners who network and support each other. It's a beautiful thing!

M I T

What's the #1 Most Important Thing I need to do right now, to help me move towards my goal?

Who have I met networking that I want to keep in touch with?

New Leads and Enquiries...

MYMM 18.

TALK ABOUT YOUR CLIENTS' SUCCESS

This is how you can really wow people at the events.

This works a treat. By sharing one of your client success stories, you're able to let the person know just how brilliant you are, *without* selling to them. Your passion will shine through.

During the story, paint the picture of what your client's experience is like from working with you.

To help you make your story succinct, use the **STAR** structure for ease.

STAR stands for Situation, Task, Action and Result. Your clients' success stories are great told in this STAR structure and you'll gain great results from talking about your STARs.

Here's the STAR structure.

Situation – What was your client's situation when they first met you? What were their main problems?

Task- What did they task you with? What did they ask you to do?

Action – How did you help them? What service or product did they buy?

Results – Importantly, what were their results from working with you?

In a moment I am going to ask you to create 3 different STAR stories. You will need to be able to share these STARs when networking, on the phone with prospective clients and in meetings as they are a great way of sharing your successes. They works so well.

Give the person in front of you, the *most relevant of examples, the STAR suited to them.*

People will then think of who else they know that had the original problem or want those results and they'll be able to recommend a contact for you.

This works well too if you ask the person in front of you to give you an example of how they've helped one of their clients.

Who do you know who you could recommend to them?

Go first. Introduce people to your new contacts and make your networking work for you and them.

Your Action Point today is to have 3 examples of recent work you can talk about and make into a STAR.

Which client success stories will you tell?

Identify and briefly write up 3 different examples of clients you work with.

Then, when you're talking to people at the event, you can talk about a *relevant* example and make a great impact.

There is plenty of space opposite to write your STAR success stories.

You can also ask these clients for a testimonial to put on your website, see page 266.

STAR Success Story 1 (first name..........................)

Situation – What was your client's situation when they first met you? What were their main problems?

Task- What did they task you with? What did they ask you to do?

Action – How did you help them? What service or product did they buy?

Results – Importantly, what were their results from working with you?

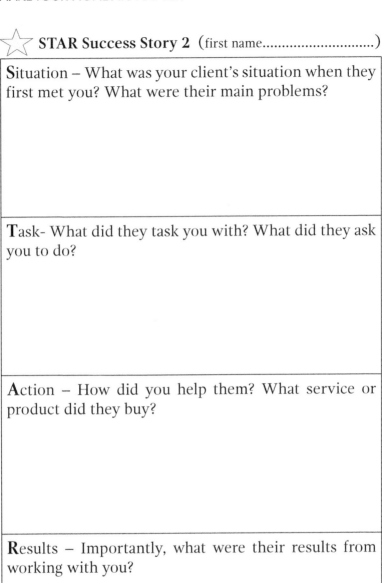

⭐ **STAR Success Story 2** (first name..........................)

Situation – What was your client's situation when they first met you? What were their main problems?

Task- What did they task you with? What did they ask you to do?

Action – How did you help them? What service or product did they buy?

Results – Importantly, what were their results from working with you?

STAR Success Story 3 (first name.............................)

Situation – What was your client's situation when they first met you? What were their main problems?

Task- What did they task you with? What did they ask you to do?

Action – How did you help them? What service or product did they buy?

Results – Importantly, what were their results from working with you?

MIT

What's the #1 Most Important Thing I need to do right now, to help me move towards my goal?

Who have I met networking that I want to keep in touch with?

New Leads and Enquiries...

MYMM 19.

GET YOUR NETWORKING HEAD ON

So, by now in Q2, you've researched the right event, you've checked out the guests' websites, you've prepared your introduction and a couple of exciting STARs, your client success stories to tell. Well done :-)

Today, let's look at getting in the best mindset for networking.

Be happy!

Put yourself in a good frame of mind before you go in and you'll find the event is more pleasurable.

Before you go, have a look at your testimonials to remind yourself of your satisfied clients.

Remind yourself of why you're running your own business.

Top Tip

Arrive wearing a smile!

Try not to moan about the public transport. Leave that at the door.

First impressions count, so breathe, shoulders back and walk in wearing that gorgeous smile of yours.

"Your smile is your logo, your personality is your business card, how you leave others feeling after having an experience with you becomes your trademark and brand."

Jay Danzie

Author, Speaker and Brand Strategist

Here's a great tip to help you develop relationships and take the next step.

Arrange to 'carry on the conversation' while you're there.

If you're interested in finding out more about someone and their business, or vice versa, get out your smart phone, open the calendar and arrange when you can speak again, or when's good to meet up.Remember to use the Alternative Close.

Then...

Add your new contacts to your social media platforms.

Sometimes you can do that while you're at the event, or afterwards.

Where does the person like to hang out online?

LinkedIn, Twitter, Facebook, Instagram? Ask them!

You can then both connect with each other. Give the person a quick tweet or post a pic of you both, or read and like some of their recent posts.

Engage with them and carry on the conversation.

Social media is like attending a networking event but it happens online.

It uses the same principles as networking and the beauty is there's so much information for you to learn from people's posts and by the very nature of it being called 'social' media, you can connect with people and importantly, *engage* with them. Chat, ask questions, be interested in them, just as you would if you were in the same room. Because in a way, you are, it's just on an online platform, not in a venue!

Is there a hashtag (#) for the event?

Other attendees will be able to find you using the hashtag, and vice versa.

If you don't connect at the event, connect *after* the event.

On your way home or the next day, find the people you were talking to and add them, tweet them or send them a LinkedIn request.

What are *their* preferred social media platforms?
Connect with them there.

This will supercharge your networking time at the event, and you can carry on the conversations and keep in touch with your networks online too. Send them a direct message.

Networking takes time and effort, so don't waste the opportunities that you have started creating.

Top Tip

The secret to successful networking is in the 'Follow Up'

Follow up with people and send them whatever you promised them.

Write an introductory email to one of your contacts if you said you would.

You will stand out from the crowd and see more results from your networking if you *follow up* more.

Remember those scary stats!

Only about 50% of people even follow up once,

25% follow up twice

and only 12% follow up 3 times.

So, be different and take the initiative to follow up more. You will make more sales this way.

MIT

What's the #1 Most Important Thing I need to do right
now, to help me move towards my goal?

Who have I met networking that I want to keep in
touch with?

New Leads and Enquiries...

My Top 10

1.

2.

3.

4.

5.

6.

7.

8.

9.

10.

My 3 Meetings this month

Date:

Name:

Contact details:

Location or online:

Any other info:

Date:

Name:

Contact details:

Location or online:

Any other info:

Date:

Name:

Contact details:

Location or online:

Any other info:

MYMM 20.

BOOK AND GO AGAIN

Seeing your network regularly and meeting new contacts each month will certainly help people to meet you, get to know, like and trust you.

This is all helping to build and develop relationships, trust in your brand, your company and YOU.

So, get out there, build your network and enjoy it. It's a wonderful way to work. Yes networking is working! But I much prefer having lunch or a cocktail with like-minded business owners, than being stuck in my office all day.

Your action point today is to book onto another networking event to attend this month and next.

MIT

What's the #1 Most Important Thing I need to do right now, to help me move towards my goal?

Who have I met networking that I want to keep in touch with?

New Leads and Enquiries...

MYMM 21.

HOW WELL ARE YOU CONNECTING WITH
YOUR WEBSITE VISITORS?

After meeting people at networking events, they are probably going to visit your website too. And of course people will also visit your website from online searches.

Are you making it easy for people to *stay* connected to you to help you nurture your relationships?

When visitors look at your website, is it obvious what you would like the visitor to do next? If they enjoyed your blog or you write a newsletter, how can they receive more great information from you?

Sometimes I see website owners making it hard for visitors, their prospective customers, to stay in touch. I hope you're not! Let's check.

Visitors will scan your home page in 3, 6, or 9 seconds (depending on which source you read!)

So check – are you making it easy for visitors to stay in touch with you or are you making it very hard? A teeny weenie sign-up box at the bottom of a page won't attract much attention will it?

I recommend you have a 'sign-up' box on your home page, or a pop-up and another 'sign-up' box at the end of each of your blog posts.

Don't hide it! Make sure it's easy to see and remember to **add the benefits to what the subscriber will get** from signing up with you.

Top Tip

Check the Data Privacy Regulations
in your country.

Are you offering your visitors and prospective clients:

➠ An e-zine/PDF download to solve one of their main problems?

➠ A video series to educate them on a specific topic?

➠ A blog or newsletter to share your expertise and inspire them?

Your Action Point today is to check people can stay connected to you online *and* **if not, update your website.**

Look at your Google Analytics and see what other pages are popular viewing after your home page. Put a sign-up box there too.

Put your sign-up box on multiple pages – on your Home page, your About Me page, at the end of each blog.

Yep, put them where your potential clients visit!

And check – is your phone number easy to spot? Yes people still want to be able to call you too!

M I T

What's the #1 Most Important Thing I need to do right now, to help me move towards my goal?

Who have I met networking that I want to keep in touch with?

New Leads and Enquiries...

MYMM 22.

IMPROVE YOUR 'ABOUT ME' PAGE

Your 'About Me' page is usually the 2nd most visited page, after your Home Page.

I interviewed one of my clients last week, as we're writing his 'About Me' page for his new website. How's *your* 'About Me' page? Have you looked at it recently? Could it do with a makeover and a refresh?

Here are 5 ways to improve *your* 'About Me' page.

1. **Is your credibility and authority clearly expressed?** As you write about your past experiences to demonstrate your credibility, pick out what's relevant to your clients' goals and objectives. We don't need to know about every job you've had! It doesn't need to read like a CV. But tell us how you got here, what challenges you faced, what you did to overcome them and give relevant information that will inspire and give confidence to your readers that YOU are the person to work with, to solve their problems, to get the results and outcomes they want.

2. **Do you need to get some new testimonials on your 'About Me' page?** Keep it fresh. Update your page with testimonials as often as you can. Your clients' words will speak volumes about your work, what you did for them, and your brilliant level of service.

3. **Is your 'About Me' page written in the first, or third person?** If you're a Solopreneur, write in the first person, using 'I'. If you run a small business with a team, say 'we'. Often I see Solopreneurs' websites written in the first person, then when I go to the 'About page', they've changed to the third person! Keep it consistent in HOW you're talking to your readers and your potential clients. You'll stay in rapport that way.

4. **Do you need a new picture?** Is it over 3 years old? You might want to get a new photo shoot done with a professional photographer. Is your picture on your website the same on your social media accounts? Don't confuse your readers, keep it consistent.

5. **What's your BIG WHY?** Why are you doing what you do? Tell us. People like to know what your Mission is. Why you're doing what you do. It speaks volumes.

So, your Action Point is to take some time today, or schedule time in your diary for later on in the week to have a look at *your* 'About Me' page.

See how you can improve your 'About Me' page. Make sure it *sounds* like YOU, *looks* like you and *inspires* your readers with confidence.

Top Tip

Have a 'call to action'
on your 'About Me' page too.

What do you want your reader to do next?

➠ Call you?

➠ Email you?

➠ Book a consultation?

➠ Sign up to your newsletter or blog?

Tell them and make their life easier, which will make YOUR life easier as your website visitors can start their relationship with YOU.

MIT

What's the #1 Most Important Thing I need to do right now, to help me move towards my goal?

Who have I met networking that I want to keep in touch with?

New Leads and Enquiries...

MYMM 23.

WHICH WAY DO YOU MOVE?
TOWARDS PLEASURE OR AWAY FROM PAIN?

How are you feeling today? Are you looking forward to the week ahead and what you're going to achieve?

Or are you feeling stuck, overwhelmed, or wondering where you're going to find the time to get through everything?

Reason I ask, is to bring to your attention the different way you felt and moved when you read the questions above. Did you connect more with what could happen this week? Or did you feel more connected when you read about how you might be feeling right now? Read it again if you're not sure!

Because, *50% of your website audience will engage with you more, if you're addressing the problems they are currently facing.*

They want to read about the situation they are in right now. Which makes your reader feel like you do understand them, as you're letting them know you are aware of the problems they face. Building trust and rapport.

Just like many more people buy painkillers when they have a headache, people want to move away from the pain they are in. And fast!

So, what about the other 50% of your website audience? They move towards pleasure. They engage more with what can be and where they want to be, in the future. Are they motivated to reach their business goals? Having your new product or service to make their lives easier?

So today, your Action Point is to check your website is addressing both the outcomes *and* the problems your customers usually have, *before* **they work with you.**

Also, when you're on the phone or in meetings, listen out for which direction your client moves in the conversation.

Do they move *towards pleasure* or away from pain?

Are they talking about how they want their team to perform or are they talking more about their problems?

Ask them, "what won't happen if you don't solve this?"

Listen carefully.

Knowing which direction your clients move in, helps you to establish and deepen rapport and will help you to solve their problems, the way they like to be solved.

When you're talking about how your services and products can help them, remember to reflect their language and movement.

Talk about how your services and products will alleviate the problems they have right now. And recap those problems and pain points.

Talk about how your product and services have helped many people in their situation to achieve the SAME goals they have.

Tell them about a Client Success Story, your [3]STARs, that's relevant to them.

Listen more to the direction your clients move, reflect this in your meetings and notice the difference it makes to your sales this Quarter.

3: MYMM 18, p151

MIT

What's the #1 Most Important Thing I need to do right now, to help me move towards my goal?

Who have I met networking that I want to keep in touch with?

New Leads and Enquiries...

My Top 10

1.

2.

3.

4.

5.

6.

7.

8.

9.

10.

My 3 Meetings this month

Date:

Name:

Contact details:

Location or online:

Any other info:

Date:

Name:

Contact details:

Location or online:

Any other info:

Date:

Name:

Contact details:

Location or online:

Any other info:

MYMM 24.

TIME TO ELEVATE YOUR PRESENCE

Start writing that blog you know deep down you want to write and share your story.

Start making that video you want to record to inspire others.

Why? Sharing your expertise with more people will help your business succeed quicker. You will be found on Google searches easier as you'll be refreshing your website regularly, and your SEO (search engine optimisation) will give you Google juice.

Your network and community online will be able to understand your expertise and you'll deepen the connections and rapport with people browsing your website which in turn will give you more leads and enquiries.

So, what valuable content can you share today?

If you're struggling or procrastinating with exactly *what* content to produce, review your [4]Features and Benefits Checklist and [5]STARs. What are the problems you help your clients with? Write a blog about it and give a solution? Give valuable content and you'll attract more of your ideal clients.

4: MYMM 3, p69
5: MYMM 18, p151

M I T

What's the #1 Most Important Thing I need to do right now, to help me move towards my goal?

Who have I met networking that I want to keep in touch with?

New Leads and Enquiries...

MYMM 25.

HOW CAN YOU IMPROVE YOUR PROFITS?

Wow, it's nearly the end of Quarter 2. This is a great exercise to complete to see how you can improve your profits at this time as you have more data to review.

I had a meeting with a lady recently and we sketched out her new business idea. We sat down and drew out the ten steps to help her make her ideas come to life and I wanted to go through her figures for growth.

There was a big silence and reality check when we looked at how many products she had to sell to get the *profit* she wanted.

It's not just all about turnover, you want and *need* to make a profit.

What can you change to improve your profits?

Two main ways to improve your profits are to either put up your prices or lower your costs. Or both!

You can work this out by taking your income and minus your costs.

It's always a good exercise to work out what your average order value is too. This gives you critical information to see whether your outgoings and costs are being effective or do you need to tweak them to help you achieve more profit?

Here's a quick way to know what your average order value is.

There's space opposite for you to work it out.

1. What was your last 3 months' income?

2. How many clients did you work with or how many products did you sell?

3. Divide answer 1 by answer 2 to get your 'Average Order Value' = the average amount your clients spend with you. Your AOV.

4. Now, how much are you spending to acquire those clients? Add up all your costs in the last 3 months.

Tracking your money is an important element of your business. Make sure you've more coming in than going out each month. If it's the other way round, things need adjusting, fast!

Can you see where you can reduce your costs or see where you could improve your average order value?

It could be as simple as arranging to meet new prospects and clients on the same day to save money on travel or parking.

The more you track and understand your financial situation, the more knowing your figures will help you have a more profitable business = more dividends and income for you!

Do this exercise with Q1 and Q2 and notice how your AOV has improved or work out what needs to change to improve it. Then repeat and tweak in Q3 and Q4 for maximum results.

My AOV for ...

Q1.

Q2.

Q3.

Q4.

MIT

What's the #1 Most Important Thing I need to do right now, to help me move towards my goal?

Who have I met networking that I want to keep in touch with?

New Leads and Enquiries...

MYMM 26.

DATE:

REVIEW YOUR PROGRESS

You are now 6 months into the year. It's time to review your progress.

This is the end of Q2 and before you head into Q3, I invite you to find some time today to reflect and focus on the results that you have gained in these last 3 months. The most successful business owners do this. You want to know where all your time, efforts and energy have been most effective, don't you? Good.

Taking time to work on your business today will help you gain more results in the future.

Let's go!

Are you pleased with your results for Q2? If so, give yourself a pat on the back, well done.

➠ What did you do, specifically, that worked really well?

➠ What do you need to do differently to achieve Q3's goals?

➠ What daily habits do you need to change to help you achieve your goals?

Write your answers in the space over the page.

What did I do that worked really well, specifically?

What do I need to do differently to achieve Q3's goals?

What daily habits do I need to help me achieve my goals?

I realise I talk a lot about taking action and reviewing what you've done regularly, but that's because taking the right kind of action is going to make the difference to you achieving the business and lifestyle you desire this year and in the years to come. I don't know of many people that have got rich by not doing much or putting things off, do you?

Keep taking steps towards your goals and you'll get there.

Let's see in more detail how you got on in Q2.

> REMEMBER
> the AmberLife #1 Business Growth Rule is
> **"Repeat what works, tweak what's not, or ditch it"**

So, first, let's look at what worked well for you and your business results. Have a look at your Top 10s, your calendar and invoice totals so far. Look at what worked, tweak what needs adjusting to improve your results, or if you have been working with certain things for 6 months now, or more, and they haven't worked at all, ditch them.

Reflect on these 7 Business Boosting Questions

1. What sales activities gave you results? E.g. How many business meetings did you have? Check the ratio of meetings to business won. How many calls did you make and what results did you gain?

2. What marketing activities gave you the leads that converted to new business?

3. Who recommended new business contacts to you? – have you thanked them? Can you reciprocate?

4. What networking events have you found? What introductions have developed into new business?

5. What blog titles or newsletter subject headers gave you the highest open rates, shares, engagement and importantly, enquiries?

6. Was there something new you did that gave you the results you were looking for?

7. How do you *feel*? An important piece of evidence to be aware of. Happy, satisfied, confident? Or do you need to change your thinking to change how you feel?

   If you're feeling frazzled or frustrated, head on into Q3 where we will talk more about developing a good business mindset to help you achieve your goals and enjoy the journey more. I'll give you a boost and you'll feel fantastic and raring to go again!

Looking again at Q2, what *are* you pleased with? Pick one thing you are most proud of. You can write in the box below.

One thing I am most proud of ...

Time to treat yourself now! This is VERY important. If you had a good boss, they would reward you for your results. So, now you need to do it for yourself.

Please take some time to reflect on Q2, especially now while it's all fresh in your mind. You can use the template on page 191 to record your achievements.

Reflecting on what has worked will give you a good boost and show you clearly what to **repeat, tweak or ditch.**

Top Tip

Remember to eat those carrots
and get into the habit of recognising
what you've achieved more often.

M I T

What's the #1 Most Important Thing I need to do right now, to help me move towards my goal?

Who have I met networking that I want to keep in touch with?

New Leads and Enquiries...

My Achievements in Q2

1.

2.

3.

4.

5.

6.

Well done from me, you rock!

QUARTER 3

MAKE YOUR MINDSET MATTER
AND Q3 GOALS

STEP
UP

MYMM 27.

GET FOCUSED FOR QUARTER 3

High achievers focus on implementing systems for success. Not just external systems like sales processes, marketing, automation, etc, they focus on their internal systems for success too.

Your internal systems include how you speak to yourself as this can highly influence your outcomes. It's your mindset and perspective that super-charges you to achieve more, with ease. With this in mind, enjoy enhancing your self-belief and creating your business mindset to feel more confident.

> REMEMBER
> the AmberLife #1 Business Growth Rule is
> **"Repeat what works, tweak what's not, or ditch it"**

It's important to keep your goals in mind and maximise summer opportunities if you don't want to suffer a slump in business come September or October.

Don't let summer pass you by. Not everyone goes away on holiday or needs to have more time off over school holidays. Summer can be your busiest time.

So, it's time to set targets for the next 3 months, Q3, July to September.

Let's go!

What's important for you to have achieved in Q3?

Give yourself a monetary target for each month. If that feels comfortable to you already, add another 10% or 20%. S-t-r-et-c-h yourself. That's why they're called stretch targets.

Month 1 target:

Month 2 target:

Month 3 target:

To help you achieve your Q3 goals, check...

➠ Have you diarised a Power Hour of Sales Conversations twice a week?

➠ Make time to connect, listen, learn and develop your relationships.

➠ How many networking events do you need to attend in Q3?

➠ How many client meetings did you convert to new business in Q2? Knowing that, how many do you need to book for Q3?

➠ What online sales activities do you have planned?

➠ Who do you want to meet?

And of course reward yourself for reaching or beating your targets. I love a reward. I bought myself a beautiful Cartier Tank Ring when I had made a good profit in my first business at the end of Year 1. Since then, I nearly always wear it at work as it reminds me of what I've achieved. A great anchor to boost my mindset when I look at it. What reward will you give yourself?

Here are 3 Top Tips to help boost your summer sales.

1. **Help your clients to plan ahead.**

   If some of your clients and contacts are going on holiday soon, find out who, and what you can help them with, before they go.

   Consider: What do they need to have in place by the end of summer, for September, and how can you help them achieve that? You can work on their projects while they're away so find out 'what is the next critical step' for them.

   In return you'll have new projects to work on yourself = invoices to send.

2. **Have a look at your diary**

   If you're going away on holiday, call some of your contacts before you go; either prospects, clients or people in your network, and arrange at least 3 meetings.

   Imagine how good that will feel when you get back from holiday all relaxed and you open your calendar to see meetings already booked in = Potential new business on the horizon.

3. **Remember, not everyone goes away!**

   Get in touch with clients you've not spoken to for a while and see what they need from you next. Use the fact they might be going away as a reason to call them. Find out what they need and pick up some new summer projects.

If you are going away I have 5 Top Tips to help you prepare before you go, so you can sit back and relax.

These tips also help if you need to change your schedule to fit around school holidays.

1. Are you going to respond to emails while you're on holiday? Or are you employing a VA to track your emails, respond to clients while you're away?

2. Are you going to have a social media holiday too? Or are you going to schedule your posts in Buffer, or similar?

3. What project work can you delegate to your VA or members of staff?

4. Have you put your out-of-office reply on your emails with alternative contact details for any urgent requests?

5. Plus Top Tip: Put a link to one of your popular blog posts in your out-of-office reply and see what responses and leads you receive. All while you're on holiday!

Make your Mondays matter, keep your momentum for Q3. Make it happen.

MIT

What's the #1 Most Important Thing I need to do right now, to help me move towards my goal?

Who have I met networking that I want to keep in touch with?

New Leads and Enquiries...

My Top 10

1.

2.

3.

4.

5.

6.

7.

8.

9.

10.

My 3 Meetings this month

Date:

Name:

Contact details:

Location or online:

Any other info:

Date:

Name:

Contact details:

Location or online:

Any other info:

Date:

Name:

Contact details:

Location or online:

Any other info:

MYMM 28.

RECONNECT WITH YOUR PURPOSE

Why oh why?

Sometimes when you're stressed or having one of those moments when it's not going according to plan, you may find yourself wondering why you started your business in the first place. Sound familiar? It's tough. It's challenging at times. But we need to pick ourselves up and carry on with **determination, passion and purpose**.

When you think big, bigger than yourself, it's so motivating and gets your passions stirring again.

One of my clients from years ago, Katie, is a trainer, who helps schools maximise their grants and trains teachers to be more effective when teaching vulnerable children.

Picture the *end result of her expertise* – all those children who will get the opportunity to receive a better standard of education, which will improve their relationships, communication and fundamental skills which will give the children such a better start in life and a much brighter future.

The purpose of Katie's business has such an impact on so many people in so many ways. Inspiring. Full of purpose.

So your Action Point today is to remember your *purpose* **for starting your business.**

Remember *why* you are doing this and take a moment now to think about that again.

Who are you doing it for? Yes, of course this may include your personal goals too.

Who gains as a result of your expertise?

Picture all the people that you are helping and supplying with your gorgeous products and excellent services, doesn't that make you proud?

Doesn't that make you sit up again and say, yes, that's why I do it?

Isn't that motivating?

Feel that drive and have a great day.

Go sparkle!

MIT

What's the #1 Most Important Thing I need to do right now, to help me move towards my goal?

Who have I met networking that I want to keep in touch with?

New Leads and Enquiries...

DATE:

FEEL-GOOD GOALS

We're going to add a feel-good goal into your day now to help you take action and make it happen.

My feel good goal is to be excited.

There's no point setting yourself a target if you're going to be completely stressed out trying to get there, or *only* being happy *when* you've got there. We don't like that! Of course, set monetary goals. You need to know where you're heading and have targets so you can tweak your performance over the weeks and months ahead to improve your results and hopefully, meet and exceed your monetary goal.

It's the journey that counts too. So set *feel-good* goals, not toxic goals.

It will be so much better if this time next year you get the monetary results you want *and* you're feeling relaxed, pleased with the amount of effort you put into making your business a success, and smiling. That's a much better picture of you, isn't it?

So, your Action Point today is to write a feel-good goal or mantra for yourself. For example, a great mantra to have is to be kind to yourself. If you start getting stressed or you feel bogged down with it all, read your feel-good goal and find another area in your life, be it sport, visiting friends and family, going to an art exhibition or a dinner out, whatever helps you to achieve your feel-good goal. This way you're not putting everything down to your business achievements. It's not everything in your life is it? It might feel like it some days, and that's when it's a good reminder to see how you can achieve your feel-good goal too. You can use the space below to write your mantra.

Be kinder to yourself. Breathe. Relax. Feel good again. It will all be OK. Things will change. We can guarantee that!

Let's remove any blocks and fears and make the next 6 months sparkle even more. Ready?

Let's go!

My feel-good goal or mantra is...

MIT

What's the #1 Most Important Thing I need to do right now, to help me move towards my goal?

Who have I met networking that I want to keep in touch with?

New Leads and Enquiries...

MYMM 30.

DATE:

DO YOU ENJOY THE PRESSURE OR ARE YOU REALLY STRESSED OUT?

How are you coping with your increasing workload?

There's a difference between feeling naturally tired from all your hard work and feeling totally worn out due to being stressed.

From working with hundreds of business owners and noticing my own stress levels and what triggers this, I have found that pressure and stress are two *very* different things.

Pressure is having a lot to do, being able to do it and enjoying it and being aware of your results. I know many people enjoy the last minute energy and pressures of a deadline. I do. Do you?

Stress generally happens when we are just too busy being caught up being busy, doing things over and over but getting nowhere fast, getting caught up in life's details and not enjoying them. Like being on a hamster wheel. My advice? Get off quick! Recognise it and do something about it. Now.

Do you know what happens when stress builds up?

Sadly it's when illness can occur. Back aches. Neck aches. High blood pressure. Nervous breakdown. Cortisol is produced in our bodies when we get stressed. Too much and it can be potentially life threatening.

Don't delay, recognise it and act today.

We can help our bodies to combat cortisol by producing more serotonin and endorphins, the good chemicals that are produced in our bodies naturally by smiling, laughing, relaxing more and exercising.

So here's your Action Point for today...

Relax more. Find a way to relax today. And tomorrow!

Go for a walk in the fresh air. Go to the gym again. Have a massage or a swim. Or cook. Whatever works for you.

Finish an hour earlier today and treat yourself to some 'me time'. Yes, time for you. Not your clients or family, *you*.

That may sound alien to you, but you need to be in tip-top shape for your clients and family.

If you're struggling, find someone who can help *you*. There are so many people that have set up in business to help you. There are coaches, therapists and practitioners of many forms. Getting a cleaner can change your life too!

If you need help, please ask someone. You'll be helping their business too.

M I T

What's the #1 Most Important Thing I need to do right now, to help me move towards my goal?

Who have I met networking that I want to keep in touch with?

New Leads and Enquiries...

MYMM 31.

WHAT IS STOPPING YOU BEING SUPER-EFFECTIVE?

As your year gets underway and the list of things to do grows, being more mindful of your time management habits can certainly help you to be more effective and focused instead of feeling frustrated and tired by the end of each day.

Do you *start* lots of things during the day, but not FINISH them?

Running your own business, means taking on so many roles and responsibilities, there's a lot to do isn't there?

I can imagine you start off the day with all good intentions but do you sometimes find yourself saying you've *'run out of time'* or *'time has just disappeared'*? Or you reach the end of the day and you've not done the important things because you got distracted?

You've heard me say *"Taking consistent action is key to your success"*, so what's stopping you? Let's find out.

Today, notice what's *taking time* AWAY from you?

⫸ **Are you checking your phone every time it pings** or a notification pops up on your home screen? I do love using my smartphone, but I find it can suck my time too as it's so distracting! When you need to, turn your phone over and turn off the sound

211

for an hour at least, while you get those important things done. Notice the difference this makes to your productivity.

➠ **Are you spending way too long on something that could be delegated or outsourced?** Is it time to get in touch with a Virtual Assistant now to help your workload?

➠ **What do you need to say no to?** Tricky I know, but check, are you always saying yes, but never finishing things, then you feel deflated and overworked? Stop! Give others *and* yourself more *realistic time frames*. Doing things well takes a good amount of time, doesn't it?

➠ **Do you need to get up an hour earlier** to give yourself *more* time? Are you getting enough sleep in the first place, or are you running on half-empty. Lack of sleep is detrimental to our health and our focus.

So your Action Point today is to notice what's taking time *away* from your day's progress and decide to make some changes.

Claim your time as yours, more often.

MIT

What's the #1 Most Important Thing I need to do right now, to help me move towards my goal?

Who have I met networking that I want to keep in touch with?

New Leads and Enquiries...

My Top 10

1.

2.

3.

4.

5.

6.

7.

8.

9.

10.

My 3 Meetings this month

Date:

Name:

Contact details:

Location or online:

Any other info:

Date:

Name:

Contact details:

Location or online:

Any other info:

Date:

Name:

Contact details:

Location or online:

Any other info:

Let's talk about your *beliefs* around money.

You've probably heard of these before...

"Money is the root of all evil"

"Money doesn't grow on trees"

"I can never be rich"

"I can't charge that much, it's more than my competitors"

Completely untrue and not very helpful sayings, aren't they?

Where do your money beliefs come from? Are they yours?

Some of our beliefs are passed to us from our parents, teachers, and of course, the media, TV and the news. The news loves to report doom and gloom and tries to instil fear in us. I hate that, don't you? (Don't get me started, I could write about that all day long!)

Are your money beliefs helping or hindering you?

If your beliefs are currently stopping you from doing the things you want to do, question them.

Change your beliefs to help *you* more.

When I changed my money beliefs years ago to thinking from scarcity to abundance, so many things started to change for the better. More opportunities came to me and my family, and I felt more in control, relaxed and hopeful.

Your Action Point today is to take a moment now to write your new money beliefs.

Just relax and ask yourself these questions:

What beliefs around money would I rather have instead?
With this new belief, how will I feel?
Now I have this new belief, what other changes can I see happening in my business and my life?

Read your answers again. Take a deep breath and smile, so your brain knows you like it.

M I T

What's the #1 Most Important Thing I need to do right now, to help me move towards my goal?

Who have I met networking that I want to keep in touch with?

New Leads and Enquiries...

MYMM 33. DATE:

WHAT ARE YOU SAYING TO MOTIVATE YOURSELF?

Growing up, if I was stuck on my homework, I used to say, "Dad, I can't do this" (and have a little teenage strop!), to which he often replied to encourage me, "there's no such word as can't, young lady!"

Use these 3 powerful words instead and notice what happens in your day.

"Actually, I can"

Those words are empowering to me. Are you stuck on something?

What are you saying to motivate yourself?

Sometimes it's our own internal dialogue that's stopping us from getting things done. If you're saying "I *should* do x, y, z, or I *could* do x, y or z, or I *would* do x, y, z" and at the end of the day it still hasn't been completed, stop for a moment and make a conscious change to the language you're using.

Replace your shoulds, woulds and coulds with **"I can"**, or **"I will"**, or **"I'm going to"** or **"I want to"** and feel yourself being naturally more motivated towards the task in hand.

My mum and dad owned a hair salon, which is where I grew up and worked during holidays and Saturdays.

Working on reception was where I learned that being the first point of contact with customers is so important to the experience they have and the picture they have of you as a business. They taught me well and I remember Dad's words to this day when I get stuck. It makes me smile and move on to find a solution.

So, what can you change today?

Your action point today is to review your internal dialogue. Is it helping or hindering you?

Undo your limitations by changing your internal dialogue.

Choose to change your language to help create new choices, and get the results you want to see.

Make your Mondays matter, you can do this.

MIT

What's the #1 Most Important Thing I need to do right
now, to help me move towards my goal?

Who have I met networking that I want to keep in
touch with?

New Leads and Enquiries...

MYMM 34.

ARE YOU GETTING IN YOUR OWN WAY?

I'd like to introduce you to reframing. It's a way of 'flipping' phrases around to give you a different perspective on the situation. This then changes how you feel, which will make all the difference to you and your day.

For example, I could say, "oh no, it's raining again".

The reframe, or flip, is 'it's raining again, great, that's good for the garden' which feels better, doesn't it?

Flip it to a different meaning = getting a different feeling

Flip things to get yourself unstuck, to stop negative thoughts and negative feelings.

You'll find solutions more quickly and easily, allowing you to get on with your day again with more positive outcomes.

Your action point today is to notice where you can flip something that you say, to help you *feel* better.

Is there a phrase that you often use when you're feeling blue? Flip it to feel in the pink. It works wonders when working with teams and clients too.

For example, if they start telling you what a bad day they are having, reframe or flip it with "it's a good job

222

I'm calling you now to help you" or if they say "this just seems impossible for me to do today" flip it with "let's sort this out together now, I'm sure between us, we can work it out". They'll feel better immediately and you'll get the job done. #Result.

➤ **Flip It and Move On** ◄

➤ **Flip It and Feel Good** ◄

It works a treat.

Have a flipping good day!

Nerves or excitement? What's in a name?

When running your own business, you have so many things to do that are *new*, don't you? You are in situations that are challenging and you are made to step out of your comfort zone on a regular basis.

But it's by *doing* things that you learn so much and your confidence grows as you find out that actually, when you've done it, it wasn't as scary as you thought in the first place. You're still standing. You made it.

But maybe you felt nervous sometimes beforehand. If you've ever walked into a room full of people and you feel slightly jittery or you get butterflies in your stomach and you're breathing a little faster, you're probably experiencing a surge of adrenaline. It can help us, but sometimes it hinders us. And it's all due to how we look at it and what we name it.

Nerves or excitement?

Adrenaline is a hormone produced during high stress *or* exciting situations. I know which I'd rather have!

223

Before I started AmberLife, in my recruitment agency, I helped hundreds of people prepare for their interviews and hone their presentation technique so they got the jobs and careers they wanted.

Interviews, meetings and networking are similar situations where your body might trigger a quick burst of adrenaline.

So, to help you, first choose what you name it!

Instead of nerves, name that feeling as 'excitement'. And notice the difference that makes already.

Enjoy the extra energy it gives you, use it to your advantage and it will help you get the results you want. Now, where and when will it be more useful for you to feel excited instead?

As I said to my candidates...

"Nerves? No, it's only a bit of adrenaline. You're excited because you want this job.

Now, take a deep breath, in and out, be proud of who you are, shoulders back, head held high, smile and enter the room.

Go and wow them. Go sparkle"

And they did. Now you can do it too.

MIT

What's the #1 Most Important Thing I need to do right now, to help me move towards my goal?

Who have I met networking that I want to keep in touch with?

New Leads and Enquiries...

MYMM 35.

POWER UP YOUR PRODUCTIVITY

Change your day around to improve your results.

Do you need to change *when* you do things during your day?

Are you trying to cram in doing your client work, networking, marketing, sales and blog writing ALL into one day, but not finishing things and getting stressed, or worse, deflated?

If you're doing the same thing and getting the same results and you're *not* happy with the results, switch things up a bit.

By completing your MIT earlier in your day, it will send a good positive feedback loop to your brain, giving you more energy and drive to tackle the next MIT. It really works. If you want to recap your MITs, have a look in the Get Organised and Get Started section of this book on page 54.

Here are some ways you can switch things up! Try them on for size, see which fits, what suits you best? For example,

1. **Do your Most Important Thing for your business FIRST.**

   Rather than reacting and responding to emails when you sit down at your desk, or drawn into something that drains your energy by 9.30am, do *your* #1 MIT first. Try not watching the doom-and-gloom news in the morning completely and notice the difference in your mood and your ability to get more done in the mornings. This particular change, not watching the news, had a *massive* effect on what I completed by midday. Try it!

2. **Schedule your meetings differently**. Leave the house earlier and arrive at your first meeting by 8am and have a coffee instead of a lunch meeting (which eats into your day, excuse the pun!) Giving you more hours to get **the next MITs done** after your meetings finish.

   Or schedule 3 or 4 meetings all in one day. You'll be on a roll too as your confidence will grow during the day. Try it!

3. **When can you have more video calls instead of travelling?**

   This is a great way to catch up with people from your networking groups and having that one-to-one meeting. It's like being in the same room, and you'll SAVE hours of time allowing you more time in your day to get on with more client work and your MITs.

   Instead of a one hour meeting becoming a 3-4 hour meeting if you include travelling time, hop onto a Skype call, or Facetime, WhatsApp video calls, whichever you prefer to use.

What else do you need to change around in your day to help you achieve more?

This might seem obvious to switch things up, and it might take time before it becomes a new habit, but like anything worth having, stick with it.

Commit to it. You'll get your MITs done regularly and will be ahead of the game, taking consistent action in growing your business. Imagine how good that will feel.

So today, your Action Point is to take some time to see if you can change the time you do your MIT to improve results.

Do it, before anything else. Switch off all distractions. Focus and get it done. Feel good.

Top Tip

Developing muscles takes a little time, so maintain your new routine for the next four weeks and then assess your results. Notice what you notice along the way. Make a few notes so you can reflect later and see your results and improvement.

MIT

What's the #1 Most Important Thing I need to do right now, to help me move towards my goal?

Who have I met networking that I want to keep in touch with?

New Leads and Enquiries...

My Top 10

1.

2.

3.

4.

5.

6.

7.

8.

9.

10.

My 3 Meetings this month

Date:

Name:

Contact details:

Location or online:

Any other info:

Date:

Name:

Contact details:

Location or online:

Any other info:

Date:

Name:

Contact details:

Location or online:

Any other info:

MYMM 36.

PERFECTION IS PROCRASTINATION'S EVIL TWIN SISTER

Are you using perfection as an excuse?

You must have heard someone else saying that they can't show you something because it's not *quite right*, or they're saying it's not finished because it's not *quite perfect*?

Get out of the perfection trap. Quickly.

This is a trap you want to stay clear of, otherwise it will really get in your way and stop you from taking those all-important next steps and it seriously hinders your creativity.

Perfection is procrastination's evil twin sister!

If you strive for perfection, settle for excellence.

Get out that piece of marketing material, blog, website page, social media post or story. Check for typos and grammar, of course, but if you've been sitting on a piece of work for a while now, I recommend you give it one last look over, one last edit and then do it. Press the send button. Press publish.

Otherwise no one will ever know about it anyway. And if you don't act fast, someone else just might do it before you, and then you'll be frustrated you didn't do it, won't you? And all that time and effort you spent on it. I won't go on, you know what I mean. You can do it.

I bet it's excellent, isn't it?

Now get it out there, show us and make some sales.

M I T

What's the #1 Most Important Thing I need to do right now, to help me move towards my goal?

Who have I met networking that I want to keep in touch with?

New Leads and Enquiries...

MYMM 37.

DATE:

HOW MUCH TIME DO YOU SPEND WORRYING?

Anxiety is often caused by 'worrying in excess'.

Generally, worrying is started by negative self-talk, imagining the worst of situations. Then quickly followed by asking yourself a string of negative 'what-if' questions, which completely exacerbates the problem and you end up feeling worse, deflated, and more worried. And sometimes ill.

But, how much of what you worry about comes true?

Out of ALL the things you have worried about in the last 2 months, name 10 things that have actually become reality.

Difficult huh? I bet you're having a tricky time coming up with 2 or even 3 aren't you?

Worrying is only a habit. As we know that we are generally causing the worry by our negative thinking, we can choose to change it. So the good news is you can wave goodbye to that habit and create some new ways of thinking to help you instead.

Get a new good habit. One where your thinking will help you feel so much better, more in control and calmer which will alleviate your stress and anxiety. That would be good wouldn't it?

235

Choose one of these today:

1. Is the worry caused by procrastinating? You would really benefit by spending some time to work out what you can *do* about the situation instead. Identify the MIT you can do right now to move you towards your goals. If you're feeling really stuck and can't work it out yourself, ask for some help.

2. Instead of 'worrying' flip it and change it to 'wondering' instead. Wondering is still thinking about things that haven't happened, but in a more positive way. It's when the what-ifs actually *turn out well*. Then what would you be able to do?

3. As worrying is caused by having *imagined it*, it never even happened in the first place, did it? So, worrying is actually a complete waste of time and you could be thinking of other much more pleasant and enjoyable thoughts and things to do.

Be Optimistic

You've heard the question:

> "Is your glass half full or half empty?"

Depending how you look at it puts you in a different frame of mind doesn't it? So we can use this to our advantage.

The good news is, *you* get to decide how you feel.

As you trigger different beliefs around what may happen depending on whether you see the glass as half full or half empty, your expectations will differ too and you'll feel, think and act accordingly.

*"If you think you can or you think you can't,
you're right!"*
Henry Ford

Change for the better and see the difference it makes.

Always imagine your glass is half full and imagine it working out well.

Importantly you will have silenced any self-critical thoughts.

Your beliefs and actions that follow now will be more positive and you will feel and certainly sound happier, as you chat to your prospects and clients. And importantly you will also feel better about how you talk to yourself.

As we tend to get more of what we focus on, it stands to reason to focus on things going well. It works a treat.

Optimism is a tool, use it!

M I T

What's the #1 Most Important Thing I need to do right now, to help me move towards my goal?

Who have I met networking that I want to keep in touch with?

New Leads and Enquiries...

MYMM 38.

BE BRAVE

Here's a challenge for you to see what difference it makes to you this week.

After you've checked your emails first thing to see if there's something vitally important for you to do, *close your inbox, completely.*

Close your inbox until you've done what you *need* to do.

Turn your phone over, so you can't see your notifications. Turn off those pings.

Focus on doing this for 5 days and see the difference in your productivity.

Be brave. Do what needs doing.

➤ Be proactive.
➤ Not reactive.
➤ Be in charge of your own emotions.
➤ Not being sucked into the news, or Facebook, or your favourite social feed that's crying out for your attention.
➤ Start your day by putting YOUR business first.
➤ Your goals. Your business. You.
➤ Start with a smile.

Write down what you achieve. Monitor how you feel too.

Keep a journal or write in this book for the next 5 days (you'll find some blank pages at the end of this section) and note how you felt by coffee time, lunchtime, at the end of the day. How were your energy levels?

OK, I hear you, things will happen that are not under your control. So, monitor that too. Notice what 'got in the way' of you doing exactly what YOU wanted to do. If you find yourself getting pulled off course, what was it? How often did it happen? How did it make you feel?

Mindset is key to success.

Keep your Q3 end goal in mind and focus on what you want to finish, who you want to get in touch with, or who you need to follow up with regarding that proposal you're waiting to be signed off, or send those end-of-month invoices. Write down here *the* important thing that you want to see finished:

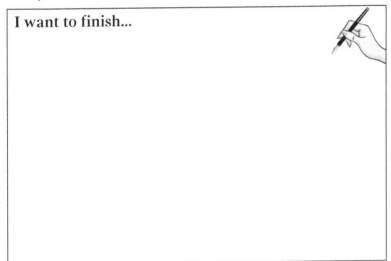

I want to finish...

You can do this. You've got this.

Remember a time now when you felt really determined.

Where were you? What were you saying to yourself? How did you feel then? Remember that time now or imagine how it would feel.

That's it, you've got it, now feeling that extra boost of determination inside you, see yourself finish what you've started. And *feel* how good you *will* feel when you have.

Choose the most important thing for you to finish today feeling good.

My 5 Day Journal
DAY 1

My 5 Day Journal
DAY 2

My 5 Day Journal
DAY 3

My 5 Day Journal

DAY 4

My 5 Day Journal
DAY 5

MIT

What's the #1 Most Important Thing I need to do right now, to help me move towards my goal?

Who have I met networking that I want to keep in touch with?

New Leads and Enquiries...

MYMM 39.

REFLECT ON YOUR Q3 GOALS AND GET READY TO ROCK Q4

Decision makers are at their desks thinking of their targets for the rest of the year and wondering how they are going to achieve them. That's where you can help them, and also help yourself and your business to maximise the opportunities this time of year brings. Provide your services to help them provide theirs.

First, I invite you to take some time to reflect on what's worked really well for you this year so far and tweak what's not!

Your Action Point is to identify your best two profit-making activities.

You can then work out how to repeat these to maximise your business in Q4.

If you can see what's not working, then I suggest it's time for a change. If you could change one thing now to help you achieve your goals, what would that be?

Keep your eye on the big picture, feel motivated and go for it.

I also invite you to take a look at the income you have already achieved so far this year and make a note of where your main successes have come from.

For example, has *most* of your business come from any of these:

➤ client referrals

➤ repeat business

➤ picking up the phone

➤ following up

➤ networking

➤ your favourite social media platform

➤ email marketing

➤ face to face meetings

➤ speaking at events

➤ blogs

➤ Where?

Then with the knowledge of knowing where your successes have come from, plan your business boosting activities with more clarity and confidence for the next 3 months.

You may need to increase some activities to ensure you meet and exceed your annual targets. So take some time to reflect on what has worked well so far and adjust accordingly.

> REMEMBER
> the AmberLife #1 Business Growth Rule is
> **"Repeat what works, tweak what's not, or ditch it"**

Make your Mondays matter and the results will follow.

My best two profit making activities...

Income I've achieved so far...

Where my main successes come from...

What I need to repeat, tweak or ditch...

M I T

What's the #1 Most Important Thing I need to do right
now, to help me move towards my goal?

Who have I met networking that I want to keep in
touch with?

New Leads and Enquiries...

My Top 10

1.

2.

3.

4.

5.

6.

7.

8.

9.

10.

My 3 Meetings this month

Date:

Name:

Contact details:

Location or online:

Any other info:

Date:

Name:

Contact details:

Location or online:

Any other info:

Date:

Name:

Contact details:

Location or online:

Any other info:

My Achievements in Q3

1.

2.

3.

4.

5.

6.

Well done from me, you rock!

BELIEVE
AND
ACHIEVE

QUARTER 4

MAKE YOUR YEAR MATTER
AND Q4 GOALS

MYMM 40.

FINISH THE YEAR STRONG AND
SET YOURSELF UP WELL FOR NEXT YEAR

The last Quarter of the year is here, so let's crack on and see what you can achieve. I'm with you, are you ready to make your dreams come true?

What do you need to do to meet or exceed your annual targets?

I'm going to give you some more sales superpowers to transform your results in Q4.

Superpowers to finish the year and to smash this year's goals and finish strong. You can do it.

> REMEMBER
> the AmberLife #1 Business Growth Rule is
> **"Repeat what works, tweak what's not, or ditch it"**

Here are 3 questions to help you gain more results in Q4. You can write your answers in the space on page 261.

1. What worked well in Q1, Q2 or Q3 that you can repeat in Q4 to get more results like that? For example, where did your best leads and ideal enquiries come from? See your achievements on pages 131, 191 and 254.

2. What tweaks do you need to make to improve your results even more? For example, how can you improve your conversion rate from an enquiry to a 'yes'?

3. What do you need to stop doing? If it's really not working, isn't it time to stop doing x, y or z? You'll then gain the time and energy to welcome in something new, or tried and tested, that does work!

We went to a beachside restaurant last week, and saw this beautiful sunset. It took a few attempts, but I got the shot! ...

Algarve Sunset, Portugal

..which reminded me of that famous quote:

"You miss 100% of the shots you don't take."
Wayne Gretzky

So, to help you take those shots, I'm here to help you.

To reach *your* targets, take some time today and work *on* your business.

What worked well in Q1, Q2 or Q3 that I can repeat in Q4?

What tweaks do I need to make to improve my results even more?

What do I need to stop doing?

MIT

What's the #1 Most Important Thing I need to do right now, to help me move towards my goal?

Who have I met networking that I want to keep in touch with?

New Leads and Enquiries...

MYMM 41.

CHECK YOUR FIGURES

The last quarter of the year is often very exciting. Opportunities that have been bubbling away come to fruition. People decide they want and need you now. And sometimes it's a tight timeframe to get it all done by the end of the year.

How are you getting on compared to your goals and income you want to achieve this year? **Here are 3 Action Points this week** to go up a gear if you need to.

1.   What £ figure do you need to achieve by the end of the year?

     Write it down here.

     I want to achieve...

     ... by the end of the year.

2.   Refresh your Top 10 today.

     Look at adding some larger organisations you'd love to work with. When you set your intention, things happen. Who do you know in any of those organisations that could introduce you to decision makers?

Talking of financial goals, today's a good day to refresh your finances.

3. Have a look at your invoices.

   Do you need to issue new invoices before the end of the year? Do you need to do a little credit control and send a polite reminder of any outstanding invoices?

> **Top Tip**
>
> In the run up to the festive season,
> keep an eye on your cash flow.

Check your cash flow as Christmas is a popular time for people to go away and not everyone is back at their desks in the New Year until mid-January.

M I T

What's the #1 Most Important Thing I need to do right
now, to help me move towards my goal?

Who have I met networking that I want to keep in
touch with?

New Leads and Enquiries...

MYMM 42.

TESTIMONIALS TALK

People love reading testimonials. They influence decisions and help people to decide to work with you. Testimonials are social proof – clear evidence that your services and products solve problems and achieve results. They are there for potential customers to read, before they make their decision to work with you, sign up, make an enquiry with you or leave your website and continue on their search.

Testimonials need to give your ideal clients that beautiful feeling of being reassured YOU can help them.

Here are 4 questions to include in a framework for a reassuring testimonial. Ask your customers:

1. What was your challenge, problem or situation before you started working with me? – this way readers can connect with the same or similar problems they are experiencing and they don't feel alone.

2. What part of the service have you enjoyed the most? – giving the reader an insight into how YOU work with your clients and the service they will receive.

3. What results have you gained from working with me? – Hard facts and evidence gives the reader hope it can happen to them too.

4. Any other comments you would like to share? Always give the opportunity for them to freely write what's on their minds and I expect you'll be pleasantly surprised with what they have to say.

You can use these questions if someone asks for help in how to write a testimonial for you.

Check with them they are happy for you to include their name and business name. Not everyone wants to include their name, so if not, ask if you can include their initials, job title or industry they work in, as your readers usually connect with like-minded people.

The testimonial needs to inspire others when they read it.

The reader needs to be able to relate to the problems and can clearly see the results your clients have gained by working with you. Reassuring them YOU are the person to work with, to help them achieve and succeed.

When you receive your testimonials put them on your website. Maybe take a quote and put it on the back of your business card, on your email signature, on a social media post.

Your Action Point is to request 3 testimonials today from recent work you have completed.

Repeat every Quarter too so you are always refreshing your website with new testimonials and you'll have new success stories, your [6]STARs, to share when networking and during your sales conversations.

6: MYMM 18 p151

MIT

What's the #1 Most Important Thing I need to do right
now, to help me move towards my goal?

Who have I met networking that I want to keep in
touch with?

New Leads and Enquiries...

MYMM 43.

ARE YOU TELLING YOUR STORY ENOUGH?

As well as listening to your client's story, it's your STAR stories you need to tell in your meetings too.

It's how you've solved the problems for your other clients that your prospects want to hear about.

Using testimonials that demonstrate your success stories will help you,not only, with creating interest and desire to work with you, they also help you overcome objections before they arise. Awesome, right!

So go on, don't be shy!

Your Action Point today is to tell the people in ALL your meetings how you helped someone with similar problems to them.

That's the story they want to hear from you.

When listening to metaphors, you can't help but put yourself in the story. So as your prospects hear your success stories, a bond is created, and you gain their trust by being YOU.

As you allow yourself to tell your stories, your STARs, more opportunities will lead to you consistently winning more business.

My Top 10

1.

2.

3.

4.

5.

6.

7.

8.

9.

10.

My 3 Meetings this month

Date:

Name:

Contact details:

Location or online:

Any other info:

Date:

Name:

Contact details:

Location or online:

Any other info:

Date:

Name:

Contact details:

Location or online:

Any other info:

MAKE
IT
HAPPEN

MYMM 44.

A 15 POINT CHECKLIST TO WIN BIG CONTRACTS

As your confidence in business grows, you'll probably be looking to work with larger organisations, maybe in the public sector, charities or with corporate clients. In my experience there are a lot more hoops to jump through before you start working with them.

Here are my 15 Points to consider when pursuing big contracts with large companies and organisations:

1. **Prepare** more, they work to more rules!

2. When you're talking to them, you need to be more prepared and **pro-active** with your questions. Write out *exactly* what you need to know about working with them.

3. Find out, what's the **process** of working with them?

4. Do they have a **PSL**, a preferred suppliers list? If so, when do they review it? How can you be included on the PSL?

5. Is there a **Procurement** team? Do you know them? Check LinkedIn and see if there's anyone in your network who can introduce you to members of the team.

6. Will you be asked to put forward a **proposal** on how you'll provide your services? Do be careful not to put everything in your proposal, otherwise it's free consultancy!

7. When in the process can you make a **presentation** to demonstrate your skills, experience and suitability for the contract?

8. Be **Persistent.** Yes it may take a while longer going through their process, sometimes this can take months, so your persistence and perseverance will be needed, and your...

9. **Patience!** And importantly,

10. Think about being in **Partnership** with them. Do they have the same values as you? Will they be a good client to work with?

11. Will the margins be **profitable**?

12. When will you get **paid**? Is it on a 30 day, 60 day or 90 day turnaround after you submit your invoices? Best to know this way in advance so you can control your cash flow. Especially if you're working with freelancers who will want to get paid for their contribution.

13. So much to consider isn't there, so **plan ahead** and the process will be easier for you as you'll be more prepared.

14. Remember to be **proud** of what you can offer them – your skills, talents and experience you have are unique.

15. When talking about your **personal** service with them, describe how your service is different. How will you help make their lives easier?

Use this 15 point checklist to help you prepare and win new clients. I want you to feel confident, so they can't resist working with you!

Prepare ahead for a big win!

M I T

What's the #1 Most Important Thing I need to do right
now, to help me move towards my goal?

Who have I met networking that I want to keep in
touch with?

New Leads and Enquiries...

MYMM 45.

WHAT DOES YOUR DIARY LOOK LIKE FOR JANUARY?

November is a busy month and often decisions are made that affect the whole of next year.

My VIP Business Coaching clients and Mastermind Group clients are regularly securing new business for client projects months ahead. I'm like a very proud Aunty! They've worked so well again this year. I love their commitment, how they've grown in confidence and have doubled and trebled their income. Brilliant results.

Wouldn't it be great if you could already see a few meetings lined up for next year with your existing and potential clients?

Just imagine walking into your office next year, having a look at your diary and seeing appointments galore, set up already. Wouldn't that feel good?

So start planning for next year now to really kick-start your year.

Now's the time to get in touch with those contacts you've recently made and those you've been meaning to call and want to catch up with again.

You will stand out and be different if you do this.

And win new client work.

QUARTER 4: MYMM 45.

My clients love this and are so relieved and grateful they took the time to do it. They always win new business in January from the meetings they arranged. It's a great present for your business.

So your Action Point today and your focus for the next couple of weeks is to take the next step and invite people to meet early next year.

➠ Set yourself a target.
➠ This month book in at least 5 appointments for January, and the results will follow.

It will be a lot easier doing this now, rather than waiting 'til January when you and your clients are trying to get back into the swing of things too.

So, brighten up your diary and January will look hotter.

Go on, you know you want to.

MIT

What's the #1 Most Important Thing I need to do right now, to help me move towards my goal?

Who have I met networking that I want to keep in touch with?

New Leads and Enquiries...

MYMM 46.

INFLUENCE YOUR ENERGY TO INFLUENCE YOUR RESULTS

This time of year you might need an extra boost to your energy as in the northern hemisphere the daylight is shorter and winter sets in.

Energy levels in people are so different, aren't they? It seems like some people have Duracell batteries installed for 24/7 energy, and others have a more steady and measured distribution of energy during the day. And everything in between!

We pick up on other people's energy too. It's like a ripple effect in the office.

You sure know if someone is fed up or in a bad mood, don't you? Just as you notice if they're happy, or being enthusiastic and positive about what's happening.

Keep in mind your energy levels are *very* influential.

As a leader, a business owner, next time you're going into your client's office for a meeting or picking up the phone to a prospect, consider your energy levels first, what effect they may have on the results you want to create.

As Maya Angelou said so beautifully,

> *"I've learned that people will forget what you said, people will forget what you did, but people will never forget how you made them feel".*

How do you want your clients to feel? Pleased to see you? Excited about your new designs? Reassured you're the right person for them to fulfil their needs in photography, web design, financial advice, wardrobe makeover, PR, or, [enter your expertise here].

Remember, you cannot, *not* influence. Read that again, slowly. You cannot, *not* influence.

So, consider your energy levels first. How are you showing up?

What ripples are you creating? Are they fitting to the desired energy levels you want to create in your meeting?

How are you influencing your audience?

Energy up!

MIT

What's the #1 Most Important Thing I need to do right now, to help me move towards my goal?

Who have I met networking that I want to keep in touch with?

New Leads and Enquiries...

MYMM 47

As tempting as it is to start winding down for Christmas now, hold on! How about making these next couple of weeks really count and put yourself ahead of the game for next year?

Let's play a game.

When I owned my recruitment agency in the City, I used to run a team. I do miss those days, it was such good fun. I used to surprise my consultants with incentives to help boost their energy levels and results!

Being in a competitive, playful mindset sure helps you win more sales.

Many of my clients call me their secret line manager, and I'd like to invite you today to play this...

Money talks!

I used to stick a £20 note to my desk, and say, *"You can gladly take it, it's yours, as soon as you book a meeting with one of your Top 10 clients."*

What reward will you give yourself today when you book in a meeting with one of your Top 10 clients?

A bottle of Prosecco, some Belgian chocolates, a massage perhaps?

I also used to put a bottle of champagne on my desk and say: *"The first person to research and find 10 brand new contacts to explore and see if there's a fit, it's yours!"* Replace the champagne with your favourite tipple, or treat, but you get my drift.

Set yourself a target this week and a prize when you reach it.

What will it be?

Your Action Point today is to set yourself an activity goal and a prize.

MIT

What's the #1 Most Important Thing I need to do right now, to help me move towards my goal?

Who have I met networking that I want to keep in touch with?

New Leads and Enquiries...

My Top 10

1.

2.

3.

4.

5.

6.

7.

8.

9.

10.

My 3 Meetings this month

Date:

Name:

Contact details:

Location or online:

Any other info:

Date:

Name:

Contact details:

Location or online:

Any other info:

Date:

Name:

Contact details:

Location or online:

Any other info:

MYMM 48.

NURTURE YOUR NETWORK

There will be so many networking events and parties to go to at this time of year. Go and celebrate your hard work and support those who have helped you along the way.

How can you help them next year?

Your Action Point today is to book onto 2 festive events and enjoy meeting up with your network to celebrate all your hard work together.

Cheers!

Remember to stand out from the crowd and follow up with them after the event to send them what you promised and deepen the relationship. You will become a valuable person to know the more you help others.

Top Top

The secret to successful networking is in the '**Follow Up**'

M I T

What's the #1 Most Important Thing I need to do right
now, to help me move towards my goal?

Who have I met networking that I want to keep in
touch with?

New Leads and Enquiries...

MYMM 49.

TIDY UP THOSE LISTS AND RAISE YOUR RETURN ON INVESTMENT, YOUR ROI

Have you created many email lists over the year? I know I have! After creating a list for each networking event I've run this year, different lead magnets and others, my mailing lists have increased, so a serious tidy up was needed.

It feels more relaxing and more under control now my lists are tidy!

So, your quick Action Point today is to streamline your Contact Lists for your e-newsletters and regular e-mailshots to clients.

If you *haven't* got email lists to tidy, is next year the year you said you are going to start email marketing? I'd like to invite you to take some time to note how your expertise can help others.

In fact, *make a quick list* of the questions your clients most frequently ask you, and you'll have a good basis to start from.

Email marketing is for many a brilliant ROI (return on investment) in your marketing strategy, helping you gain good quality leads and work with more of the clients you *want* to work with. Sound good to you?

Let's do this!

Sign up to my email service provider *Constant Contact* (https://bit.ly/mymmbook) and become part of my community who want to learn and improve their email marketing and start writing newsletters.

In the interests of full disclosure, I do receive a small commission if you choose to sign up using the link above. There are other email providers to choose from. Whichever you choose, research well and use it. It works brilliantly to nurture relationships as you're sharing your expertise, giving valuable content and creating more points of contact over time. All helping you to generate new leads and win more business.

MIT

What's the #1 Most Important Thing I need to do right now, to help me move towards my goal?

Who have I met networking that I want to keep in touch with?

New Leads and Enquiries...

MYMM 50.

REFLECT ON THIS YEAR'S SUCCESS

What's worked really well for you this year?

Identify where, when and how you've got your best results so you can repeat them. This is how successful businesses are made.

Your Action Point today is to ask yourself these questions.

➠ What has been your most popular service or product?

➠ Who have been your best customers?

➠ How did you achieve your best results?

➠ What activities produced more business for you?

➠ What are the results you have achieved against your targets and goals this year?

Write your answers in the space over the page.

Do more of what works well next year and see more results.

I'm sure you have some customers and clients that are raving about specific products and services of yours. Maybe it's time to introduce them to other clients or people they can recommend you speak to. Ask them.

All helping you to gain new leads and take your business to the next level.

Do take time to work out what worked well. It will make a difference for you as you plan next year.

What has been my most popular
service or product?

Who have been my best customers?

How did I achieve your best results?

What activities produced more business for me?

What are the results I have achieved against my
targets and goals so far this year?

M I T

What's the #1 Most Important Thing I need to do right now, to help me move towards my goal?

Who have I met networking that I want to keep in touch with?

New Leads and Enquiries...

MYMM 51.

WHAT'S YOUR BEST SUCCESS STORY THIS YEAR?

Maybe you've launched a new service or product to compliment your business and help your ideal clients even more?

Maybe you're part of a new collaboration and have plans to bring it to life next year?

Maybe you've been juggling business, family *and* your health?

Maybe you've totally met your financial goals and are quietly doing a little happy dance there?

Write down your best success story of this year in the space opposite.

Whatever achievements you have made, big or small, remember you have been brave and brilliant. Yes, it's a pretty intense life being an entrepreneur juggling all things, so hats off to you, feel proud of your achievements and importantly all your new learnings this year. Here's a big well done from me.

Well done!

My best success story this year is...

MIT

What's the #1 Most Important Thing I need to do right now, to help me move towards my goal?

Who have I met networking that I want to keep in touch with?

New Leads and Enquiries...

My Top 10

1.

2.

3.

4.

5.

6.

7.

8.

9.

10.

My 3 Meetings this month

Date:

Name:

Contact details:

Location or online:

Any other info:

Date:

Name:

Contact details:

Location or online:

Any other info:

Date:

Name:

Contact details:

Location or online:

Any other info:

MYMM 52.

GIVE YOURSELF A ROUND OF APPLAUSE.
YES YOU

What a year you've had, well done.

Can you hear me cheering you from here?

I bet you've worked really hard and had your fair share of the joys and challenges of running your own business. You've probably rocked certain goals and celebrated some big wins, missed out on some, been frustrated by others. You've changed things, ditched things, some things may have been plain sailing whilst others have kept you up late at night. It's not easy sometimes is it.

It's been tough out there this year BUT you've survived and hopefully, you've thrived.

And you're going to get up and do it all again next year aren't you? So, just before we say goodbye,

Your Action Point for this week is to write down 3 things now that you're proud of and are important for you to remember.

Here are some suggestions to get you started.

1. What piece of work are you so proud of you want to shout about it from the rooftops?

2. What did you do this year that you may have thought impossible before? I'm so proud of you for changing and putting those limiting beliefs

behind you, taking action and doing it. Doesn't that feel amazing?

3. What's the MIT you have learned that was vital to your business growth this year? Are you going to repeat this again next year?

What have you noticed now that you will do differently next year? You can write all your thoughts on the opposite page.

One last thing

"Life moves pretty fast. If you don't stop and look around once in a while, you could miss it"
Ferris Bueller's Day Off.

Look at all you've achieved this year and give yourself a pat on the back and another cheer. You did it!

Go and buy yourself another present!

Look at all that hard work you've done. If you worked for someone else you'd probably receive a bonus or a gift. So I'm encouraging you to say thanks to yourself and treat yourself too. You deserve it.

I am immensely proud of you for working so well, committing to your dreams and recognising your strengths and learnings.

You did it! You made your Mondays matter. You rock!

Here's to another sparkling year ahead for you as you take your business to the next level, AGAIN.

To your success and happiness,
Jo James

This year I am proud of...

1.

2.

3.

I will do these things differently next year...

#RepeatTweakDitch

#MakeItHappen

#MakeYourMondaysMatter

#MYMM

LET'S CONNECT

Contact me by email at jojames@amberlife.com
or call me on +44 (0) 7968 016585

Meet other readers, come over to the Facebook group,
Facebook: MakeYourMondaysMatter.

Fancy meeting up? Join me for Contacts and Cocktails
– facilitated networking in central London:
bit.ly/ContactsAndCocktails

Contact me about joining one of my mastermind groups
bit.ly/AmberLifeMastermind

Connect with me on social media here:
Facebook: AmberLifeMindSpa
Instagram: jojamesamber
LinkedIn: jojamesamber
Twitter: jojamesamber

www.amberlife.com

ACKNOWLEDGEMENTS

With huge thanks to Mark, my darling husband, and my friends and family for listening while I've talked about writing this book for years. It all started with writing newsletters to my community of business owners in London which grew to Europe, US, Dubai and Australia. Every Monday I delivered an email to them without fail, empowering them to take action with top tips to grow their business and I'm so pleased to have created this book for you now.

Thank you to the brilliant business owners I've met networking in London, it's been great meeting you and catching up on your news and progress over the years. It sure has made business much more enjoyable having a great network around me. I don't think you can have a business without a network, and it's been an absolute pleasure getting to know you all. Thank you, here's to the next chapter.

Not to mention the fun we've had! The cocktails and the lunches and all the meetings in between.

I had a great childhood and so it's with huge thanks to Mum and Dad for being so encouraging to me as I explored different careers and directions in my life. As Dad told me "there's no such word as can't" and Mum has always told me, "if it feels good do it, if it doesn't, don't." Wise words to live by!

My brother has his own business too, First Aid Direct UK Ltd. He's a first aid trainer based in Lytham and it's been brilliant to spend more time together again as we get older and see his business go from strength to strength. He encourages me too, but in a brotherly kind of way! Thanks Trevor.

Thank you to my beta readers who received an advance copy and gave such rave reviews. It's been lovely to have everyone involved. Thank you for your time.

And big thanks to my publisher, Sarah, and her team at Goldcrest Books for their patience and guidance helping me bring my vision of this book to life.

ABOUT THE AUTHOR

With over two decades of growing multiple 6 and 7-figure businesses, Jo James is an experienced business coach. Her focus is empowering people with a variety of proven networking, sales and mindset strategies for success. Through her coaching work with entrepreneurs, executives and teams Jo has given her clients the clarity and confidence to significantly increase sales and take their businesses to the next level.

Living and working in Portugal and London, Jo is living her dream and now propels you to build the business you desire and live your best life.

NOTES

I've left you some pages here to write any addditional notes about your achievements, your goals or your ideas. There is a blank page for doodles and sketches with another page lined for text. Have fun!